ALONE
ALL IN ONE

A SOLITARY JOURNEY

LaSHAWNDA JONES

ALONE | ALL IN ONE
A Solitary Journey

Poems and other musings by
LaShawnda Jones

Harvest Books
Cultivating Faith

FIRST EDITION
Library of Congress Control Number: 2024913838
Print ISBN 13: 979-8-218-45274-2

*Dedicated to all the women who carried me as a seed,
birthed me into being and passed on their wisdom
through the generations.
I am a composite of each of you.*

Other Books by LaShawnda Jones

Author & Publisher
I AM WOMAN: Expressions of Black Womanhood in America
Desert of Solitude: Refreshed by Grace
My God and Me: Listening, Learning and Growing on My Journey
The Process of Asking for, Receiving & Giving Love & Forgiveness
Clichés: A Life in Verse
Fantasies: Wide Awake

Contributor
Go, Tell Michelle: African American Women
Write to the New First Lady

Available on
Amazon
BN.com
Harvest-Life.org/shop

Connect on Social Media
Blog
Harvest-life.org/blog

Instagram
@HarvestBooks1
HarvestPhoto1

Threads
@HarvestBooks1

Contents

Part 3: Wasted Tears. Wasted Years

Part 4: Relearning Me

Part 5: Learning to Trust Myself Again

Addendum

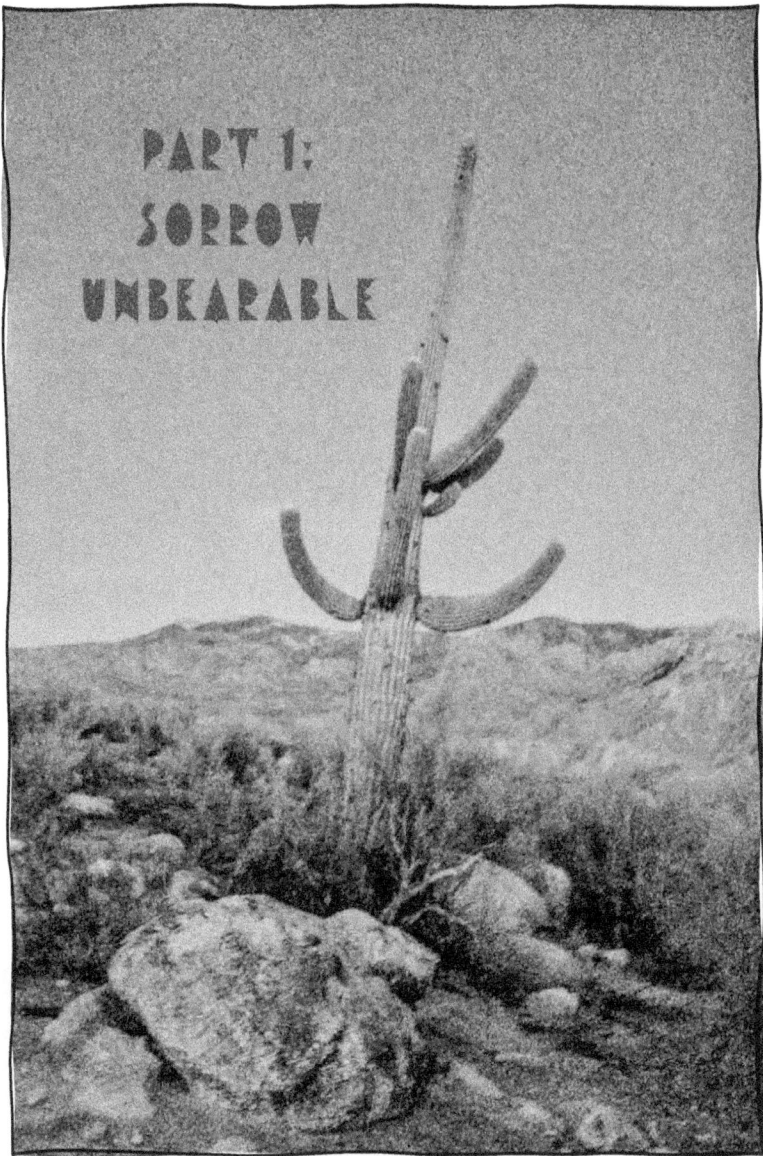

PART 1:
SORROW
UNBEARABLE

When I begged for Love

In my late twenties, I realized I was on a *Love Quest*. My mission should I choose to accept it (spoiler: I did!) was to search hungrily for people to love. The search was more difficult and labor-intensive than anything else in my life. Why? Because I tried to love everyone and not everyone knows how to be loved.

Some people beg for love. Others beg for the opportunity *to love* in hopes of reaping such devotion. I used to beg *for* love by *offering* love.

Have you ever found yourself begging someone to let you love them?

"Can I love you" seems to be the common unspoken question in all my relationships. My way of loving is giving. Giving of myself, my time, resources, energy, and attention. I open my heart, home, life, thoughts, and experiences to people. I focus on their needs, their comforts, and their situations. *"Can I love you"* is the hidden question when I ask *"What can I do for you? What will make your day better? What do you need in your life?"* I pour into them whatever I have that they may need.

When I open my ears and heart to people's troubles, I'm really asking, *"Can I love you?"* When I embrace anyone in greeting and farewell or offer to fill a need they have yet to recognize or articulate, loving them is my subtext.

"Can I love you" sounds so pathetic, I think, when heard with ears not filtered by the *Love* of God.

~ *"Can I Love You?"*
My God and Me, 2009

Internal Dialogue

What the world has taught me

People will fuck you, fuck with you, fuck you over, mind fuck you, and throw you the fuck away to show you they don't give a fuck about you. Of course, they could've just left you the fuck alone. But once you stop caring and start telling people to fuck off, you're the meanie with the fucked up attitude.

What the Holy Spirit has shown me

Everything will work to the good of those who love God without engaging in all the unsolicited fuckery people offer daily.

Where are **my** People?

Who promised **you** People?

To Be Known by No One

It must be me.
Weird. Defective.
Incomplete.
Off-putting. Irrelevant.
Unable to truly connect.
Wasted years. Deferred dreams.
Colossal amounts of
time and energy building
a life around relationships.
Weaving in love and flexibility.
Willing to be what was needed.
wherever requested
Straining to see God in the unlovable,
ungrateful and unrepentant.
Attempting to stand when
I could barely crawl.
Taking on the burdens of community
without replenishment.
Where is my shelter?
On whom can I lean?
What does a close
companion feel like?
Being fully available in
every area of life,
drains life of the Spirit.

Devoted worker –
long hours, weekends, holidays
as needed; no questions, only
willingness to adjust and give
some of me, whatever of me
all of me, when needed,
expected or demanded.
Now, there's none of me that
hasn't been discarded.

That's a me problem. I know.
I see love expressed
everywhere, every day.
People *know how* to show love.
I'm simply not a chosen recipient.
I see friendships.
People *know how* to be friends.
Unfortunately, I haven't been tagged in.
I see supportive work environments
where my labor is welcome;
but I'm excluded from the support network.
How did I get outside the matrix of life?
How did I develop outside of the norm –
on the outskirts of relationships –
when all I wanted was
to offer the best of me
to everyone I encounter?

No One Cares

No one cares about your needs.
You must care enough about yourself
to articulate and maneuver
in ways to get your needs met
despite their general lack of care.

People will look through you,
talk at you and treat you
as if you're beneath their respect,
then act clueless when you
cease engaging with them.

It's fine when they don't care about you,
But woe unto you when you stop caring
about them! Their loss. Your gain.
You deserve the best of you!

Ode to a former bestie
from her 'only darkie friend'

You must have really been something
on that island country in the Caribbean
or in the southern utopia of your mind,
where your dark caramel skin
elevated you to some delusional height,
making you think brown, but *not-too-brown*
is the best you could possibly be.
More egregious, that your skin color
automatically made you better than me.
Your haughtiness was always on display
but I filtered it through love and grace,
assuming your family's military background
gave you a worldliness my impoverished
American Midwest mind couldn't quite comprehend.

For decades, you proudly exclaimed,
"I only have three best friends!"

We claimed each other as besties in
high school, but you never let me forget
your first bestie from middle school
was a white girl in a Virginia trailer park.

Your college roommate, a white-passing
Native American was your next best friend.
She granted you lived-in proximity to the
whiteness you so desired. She elevated her rank
by introducing you to the Great White Hope, Hubby #1.

How odd I've never met Bestie Number 1.
Not at a graduation, a wedding, holiday or vacation.
Remind me, who showed up when your mom
asked for support during a medical procedure?
Not Number 1 or Number 3. Yet you gladly
travel to them *to be present* in their lives.

I remember our girlish chatter over how we would be
each other's maid of honor. Only to be told before
your first wedding, "Of course Number 1 is my maid of honor!"
Strange, I still don't recall meeting her....

The potential of Hubby #1 didn't outweigh
his emotional and medical needs. To his credit,
he warned you, family, and friends about his
limitations and boundaries. Even so,
he clearly adored you, even knowing you
held your highest appreciation for financial
potential he feared never achieving.

How does one love potential or build on it?

Ahhh.... Perhaps you began hating me....
when I advised against marrying that sweet man.
He needed far more care and support than
you've ever exhibited for anyone in your life.

I told you directly, based on your resentment
of your mother's and brother's requests of you,
you would grow to resent him.

How did I never notice, you are not fond of truth?
Have you been seething for decades while
expressing pride for a conflict-free friendship?
Until vitriol began bubbling from you.
Years later, you said calmly in conversation,
"You are my only darkie friend."
That was the first time I cursed at you.
"What the fuck do you mean "darkie?"
We were twenty-five years into a friendship, or so I thought,
before I fully acknowledged your self-hatred.

I didn't think I was in a friend category based on
skin tone. Being one of three didn't bother me.
I am unique. I know the value I add to relationships.
Not being seen as fully human, now that stung.

That was the beginning of the end of being a bestie.
A decade of winding down, a few more
cruel comments flung casually, carelessly, emotionlessly
without empathy or remorse.

The last and worst of all cruel words
were, "I don't want to," when I asked
you to simply show up, to be present for me
after I nearly died alone in my house in the desert.
I needed a friend. The only love requested was presence.
I wanted my bestie, but learned I had hater instead.

The long slow wind down became a crash landing.
I no longer cared to speak to you; had no desire
to see you. I was fine being dead to you as there
was no difference in the quality of my life.

Without grace filtering my vision, I can see
how you'd hate someone you consider inferior;
someone who didn't live down to your biases.
How dare your "darkie friend" not conform
to social pressures, while you lie to yourself
about the potential of whiteness to improve
your life. I get how the appearance of my financial
well-being would eat at someone so focused
on money and status. I understand jealousy.
I don't understand cruelty, or presenting yourself
as a friend when you couldn't care about my life or death.

It Shouldn't Take Courage to Love a Black Woman

Courage shouldn't be required to love a
Black Woman. To accept a heart given
freely or a life tribute offered with
hope of reciprocation.
                              Where is the
danger in respecting one who aches with
neglect from being habitually
dismissed and discarded through centuries
of generations?

                    What terrors does this
global shadow craft present? Projecting
false images of insecurities,
self-hate, exasperated impatience,
irrational anger, and I-got-this-
                              don't-need-you independence.
Men conjure their ideal easy woman –
hypersexuality, low moral-
                              ity, mean-spiritedness to assuage
their proclivities of abuse, torment,
separation, abandonment, lack of
support, hate, rejection, and destruction.
Women suffer from men's misplaced petty
jealousies and proud self-aggrandizement.
Society built a totem full of
grievances, animosity, blame, and
dissatisfaction, then painted it black
and shackled Black Womanhood onto this
altar where the most violent human
attacks are thrown.

                    Despite intentional
sacrilege, the Black Woman's labor is
expected without delay or complaint.
People feel entitled to her labor,
time, and presumed compliance without fail.

They assume she's duty-bound to give care;
nurture everyone else because she's
born that way – skin, gender, status. Indeed,
no part of a Black Woman's body or
existence is seen as hers to control
or use for her own purposes or goals.
Everything she is, society and
man claim to be their *droit du seigneur*.

The world delights in telling Black Women
we are nothing. We are the least desired,
our personhood is rarely valued, yet
we are always wanted for what we give.
We're only praised for productivity –
serving our way to depletion and death.

Yet ask a Black Woman who she is and
be prepared to bask in her glorious
light. We see ourselves as embodying
love, joy, comfort. We are conduits of
grace, dispensers of mercy, holders of
truth. We are Wisdom, Discernment and Guides.
We are Unbroken, Unbowed, Still Standing.
Society sees one way. We're not that.
We are not who the world says we are. We
won't perform to your low expectations.
We'll do what needs to be done, while being
who we are. We are Love, so courage is
not required to love ourselves as we are.
We're our own blueprint, goals and best teachers.

It shouldn't require courage for others
to love Black Women. We are humans with
human needs, Women with human desires.
We, too, want to be loved, cherished, honored
Respected, and held. We desire to be
accepted and embraced as we accept
and embrace others; to be Invited
into spaces so hospitable we

forget the hostility of the world;
spoken to with gentle understanding
that elicits the same kind response. We
gleefully pour ourselves into people
connected to us, even when they feed
us nothing in return. However, we,
also need to be poured into. We, too,
desire to bask in the radiance of
another's glory – to be bathed in joy,
peace and tranquility. To rest without
anxiety; wake without urgency.

We don't need grace from everyone, nor
do we expect a societal shift
in gratitude for services rendered,
but where Black Men are concerned, It shouldn't
take courage to be men of character,
substance, integrity, conviction and
discernment. To partner with Black Women
in pursuit of dignity, liberty
Love and joy without constraints. Where are the
Black Men with enough strength to support rest
for the miracle workers, shapeshifters,
gatherers, and nurturers – Black Women?

Without a doubt, each of us desires a
man who decides to follow his heart and
spirit over social conditioning
Norms, biases, and economic threats.

But alas, Black Women continue to
pray for courage to exist, keep moving,
continue showing up, to maintain our ability
to love, evolve and give grace. We pray for
respect, and a beautiful, peaceful life.

Courage should not be needed to live well
in the world. But alas, I am alone,
unwanted, loved by no one, showing up

daily for battle with resilient joy,
intent to live with radiant fervor
against all odds in a world unable
to eliminate my presence, spirit
or impact. This power is derived from
the social taboo of loving myself,
a phenomenally well-crafted whole,
proud Black Woman, without restraint, fueled
by reckless hope for a future glory.

Be Anything

I had such bright
hopes and dreams
when I believed
I could
be anything
I tried, strived
over-achieved
if thoughts
manifest reality
the American Dream
wouldn't be
unreachable
life would be
different
all I truly want
is freedom
to be me
without threat,
violence, shame or
compromise
how tragic
being me
proved to be
the hardest thing

May 24. 2023: 63 Today

Uncle Ed called to say his Big Sis would
be 63 today. Oh! How alive
that number sounds! Told him I stopped counting
at 60 for you and 45 for
me. I'm still living in 2020
it seems. It was a good year, I think.... or
maybe 60 and 45 were good
numbers for me.

It's impossible to
not remember, you're always in my thoughts,
but I worked today. This job has kept me
discombobulated. Everything is
emotionally taxing, financial-
ly insecure, physically exhaust-
ing. I'm guessing, life was the same, but more
so, for you. I know you struggled, but you
were so caring and grace-filled, it didn't
show negatively. How did you manage
life with no focused care? No time to heal
from one abusive phase to another?

Were you ever at ease? Were you ever
able to reflect and release? Did you
experience joy? What did you hope for?
How did you do it? Did you ever heal?
Had you been allowed to age, would life have
grown gentle and kind? Were gentleness and
kindness something you understood enough
to yearn for?

Your presence was joy to me.
What was joy to you? Was any portion
of your earth time enjoyable? Better
than bearable? Worthy of thanksgiving?

63 today. Each year since you left
I think I know you better than ever
and not at all. Who were you, Terry Ann?
What did you want for your life? Did you leave
unfulfilled, aching? Did you give in, just
let go of whatever kept you grounded?

Wherever you are in life after earth,
I pray you are imbued with joy, light and
all good things. I pray no memories or
shadows of your earthly sorrows travel
with you. Should our spirits meet again, I
ask only to embrace you with love and
gratitude. May the Creator of All
convey my prayer, my Beloved Mother.

Elegy: Cousin Tish - Baby Woman Mother

Playing house is different with baby
cousins, lil' brothers and sisters and the
mannish boys in the neighborhood. Who needs
a fake baby with real baby cousins
in reach? Tish was a chubby, curly-haired
infant, rosy-cheeked girly-girl toddler
adorable, rambunctious, loved. Rolling
over, pushing up learning to walk, run
circles around folks from the house and yard
to Grandma's vegetable garden; real life
cabbage patch doll blooming up and down the
street, burrowing roots, extending networks.

Too soon, I was no fun; just a boring
old cousin to a womanish girl who
preferred smokin' weed as boys circled and
plotted in her haze. Though she grew up fast,
she was no fast-tail-gal. She met her love,
married young in paradise. Soon after,
my play baby was having babies in
wedded bliss. A homemaker happiest
making a home in the warm embrace of
family, next door to her mama, 'cross
town from Grandma. A nurturing space for
herself, her husband and their one two three
four five bouncing bundles of joy. Later
expanding her shelter to make room to
comfort Grandma in her declining years.

A lifetime came and went. A final stealth
pregnancy shared with few. Heard in passing
near her due date. Her mom, my aunt, kept her
confidence; our uncle not so. She was
due on my long-deceased brother's birthday.
A happy coincidence to be sure.
On December 16, my aunt called to

check on me. She asked, "Have you gotten your
diabetes under control?" "I thought
I did, but last week I spiked," I replied.
On and on I rambled, before Cousin
Tish interrupted, "Should I let them give
Grandma the Covid-19 vaccine?" "No,"
my aunt said. "What do you think," she asked me.
"No," I agreed, "they don't know what the side
effects are." "Yeah," my aunt said, "Mom has too
many illnesses and is taking too
many medications, that vaccine could
kill her. "Ok," said the woman who was
once upon a time my play baby, as
she made arrangements for the grandmother
she was now mothering. Generations
are mere stair steps grape-vining across blurred
lines. We could've all been in the same room,
sharing the same space in momentary
unity. A rare consensus. Eighteen
hundred miles, forty years separated
us from oldest to youngest to farthest
away. "I have to go," said Auntie. "Tish
needs to get ready for the hospital.
They're inducing her tonight."
"Goodness! How does she do it all," I asked.
"What do you mean?" Intoned with a raised brow.
"She's about to deliver her sixth child.
She's on her feet to the end, taking care
of grandma, five kids and a husband. It's
a lot." With a quiet sense of affront,
my aunt said, "I help." Indeed, she does, though
not immediately apparent from
eighteen hundred miles away. As neighbors,
mother and daughter have separate but
shared households. They see each other daily.
Tish stays home, her mom works. They share the days
and divide the responsibilities.
Mini-compound in an old industry
town. How can any of us do it all

without help? "Ok, talk to you later.
Good luck to Tish." When was the last time I
told her I love her? She's kept me at a
distance for decades; I stopped trying to
bridge it long ago. What would I have said
had I known it was my last chance to speak
to her through her mom? The next morning, her
brother called to say this vibrant woman
died in childbirth. Unbelievable, yet
true. That was not the call any of us
expected to receive. From *"Good luck!"* to
"My God, may she rest in peace!" We know she
held her blessings close in a well-lived life.

Of the ways we thought any of us would
go next, the ones we were "ready" for, Tish
dying giving birth was not a concern.

Gone. Thirty-eight years young. Healthy. Happy.
Living, loving fully. Present for life.
Woman, wife, mother, daughter, granddaughter,
sister, niece, cousin, friend. Being herself
was her favorite role. *"I Am Woman.
I Am Me,"* she shared with me when asked what
womanhood meant to her during my last
visit. *"Everything about Woman
represents Me. Determination. Me
being focused. Being respectful and
making sure my children are respectful.
Having manners. Succeeding in life."* She
Will be remembered as my play baby
and a bonafide mommy-woman. She
leaves behind many impressed by all the
life in her years, her love of motherhood
all encompassing. For the little ones,
Tish's babies, overwhelming sadness
for the void her physical absence leaves
in their lives. May God enrich their spirits
to receive all the comfort, guidance and

love they need to fill their years with good life.
Precious Layla, Erick, Karess, Remy,
Daymanie and dearest London whose first
breath struggled pass her mother's last. As I
mourn Cousin Tish, I ache for the husband
she shared her life with, mother never more
than a hop away, father whose pride was
his first-born, and brother who could've been
her Siamese twin. Then there's Grandma, who
has been sustained by Tish's care and grace.
Tish, a woman who inspired by being.

Pamela Turner: Two for the Carnage of One

"Do this in remembrance of me."

It's psychological warfare
physical murder
spiritual bondage.
Our sanity means nothing
to the intentionally persistent
assassins of our humanity.
Our humanness has no value in the
confrontation of violent entitlement &
and moral disregard that assumes
murder of "others" is the
white person's right – a privilege
awarded to hunters; a prize
for the domineering.

I cried out to Jesus, only to be
consumed by His weeping and grief.
I raged at *Democracy*, only to realize
my own invisibleness.
I shouted over to my neighbors
but their thundering silence
shamed me!

I too may be America,
but what can America claim to be?
What we've become is
who we've always been.
There's no Justice in this land.
Original sin remains
throughout the encampment.
Lies, deception, greed
lead to displacement,
abduction, innumerable abominations
culminating in genocide – countless unnamed,
unmarked, unacknowledged

destroyed lives, families, connections.
Followed by more genocide to justify
imperialist colonial capitalism
domestically and abroad.
Murder of innocents by the millions.
Blood crying out from every inch of land
around the globe from the Atlantic coasts,
across the Mississippi, through Colorado,
spilling into the Pacific
beyond borders
north and south
the annihilation of seeds
birthed and unborn
the enslavement of bodies and spirits
through hundreds of generations

THEY CRIED OUT!
Those drunk on power,
intent on control, deceived
by their own malignant characters,
they can't hear the cries
from the blood they spill.
They can't see the light
of the spirits thought to be extinguished.
They can't see how the lifeforce of their
victims multiply in me. They can't perceive US.

"Why are you crying out to me?
Do something!" God shouted back!

So, I wrote this poem, even as I
continue to hemorrhage.
Blood weeping into the ground.
Invisible, unheard tears drying in air.

What comes next is in remembrance of US.
Those of US who have been annihilated.
All of US who have been decimated.
WE who have been chained and caged.

LaShawnda Jones

WE who have been disenfranchised.
The millions who have been made invisible,
intended to be forever forgotten.
WE, US, THEM, THEY, no one can forget
each of us are Fruit of the Seeds
who came before.

The gone are not forgotten.
They are embedded –
in hearts, minds, spirits.
They're still standing, united here, now.

Bound in memory, story, song and dance
Our entwined spirits remain strong.
Their seeds did not turn to dust.
They became roots.

In remembrance of ALL
the NAMES we don't know,
BODIES we haven't seen, and the
countless LIVES that continue to matter,

WE CRY OUT:
Enough!
You do not own our breath!
Leave us be!
We have a right to live!
We were created free!

Àṣẹ

Death˙ is passive. ˙Killing˙ is not.

This poem came from frustration with the passive language most media use to report state-sanctioned murder and police brutality. They say "the death of" this person or that person, as if the person died in an unremarkable way. They speak of people who "lost their life" as if the opportunity to reclaim a lost life is available. More accurate language is "a life was taken; a life was stolen; a life was destroyed by someone who had no right to take a life."

On the lynchings of Ahmaud Arbery, Breyonna Taylor, and George Floyd

There is no story attached to death.
Death is a passive word.
So-in-so died. Next line.

Kill is an active word.
Someone did something: *A killer killed.*
There's always a story attached to a killing.
    Who did the killer kill?
    How was the victim killed?
    Why did the killer target the victim?
    Is the killer still breathing?
    Will the killer be prosecuted?
    Why do killers kill?

People who kill inherently believe
they are judge, jury and executioner.
They are the law,
inhabiting space above, beyond
and around societal norms.
They enjoy an extrajudicial existence.
The law as we know it
needs to be eliminated.
We need to write new laws.
We need to establish new societal norms.

Killers need to know
murder is not something else
because of their badge,
skin color, or family connections.
Murder is an intentional act.
It is purposeful destruction of an active life.
Murderers think they have the right
To take away life.
To steal another person's breath.
To extinguish a human being's light.
They do not have that right.
They are not creators or guardians
of the Human Experience

Witnesses need to name names.
Law enforcement supervisors need to hold
perpetrators accountable for their violence,
brutality, and abuse of authority.
Administrative leave is not enough.
Job termination isn't enough.
Payouts to injured families is not enough.

Full accountability and prosecution
of murderers is necessary.
No matter their uniform.
No matter their perceived goodness.
No matter their community.
A killer is a killer. Their victims
didn't just die. They were killed.

Breath is sacred.
Breathing is active.
Air is life. We are all created beings
with the same Right to Breathe unhindered
no matter our station, status or identity.
Access to air should not depend on
assumptions, opinions, political views,
occupation, wealth, social status,
skin color, mood, hatred of fellow humans

or self-hatred. Access to air should
not require legislation.
Yet here we are.

There is a great lack
of understanding in America,
an astonishing general ignorance
across the continents,
of an elemental natural truth:

> *The deeper they grind US into the ground,*
> *the stronger OUR roots become.*
> *One day, their tsunami of brutality*
> *will wash them and their generations*
> *into the sea they brought US across,*
> *while WE who are deeply rooted*
> *in the soil, remain standing.*
> *Flourishing gloriously in the Sun.*

Lockdown. Lockdown!

How to articulate the frequency
of death's proximity juxtaposed to
the lack of care others have for others?

Post school lockdown clarity is glaring.
Security holes and safety lapses
are painfully acute, waving loudly.

Truth becomes brutal in the narrow scope
of hindsight. This day, I could've been one
of the first to die. Exposed at the front
desk, visible through two walls of glass as
I stood dialing 911. Listening
to the reporting parent describe the
man walking around the school with a gun
exposed on his hip.

                   Was he angry? Who
was he looking for? Was he a parent?
Did someone hurt his child? Was he seeking
retribution?

             The 911 person
asked for my address, "*Can you repeat that?*"
my name, "*Can you spell that?*" and perhaps my
date of birth before getting to why I
need help: *What's your emergency?*

                       "I'm at
the elementary school. A parent
reported he saw another parent
walk to the back of the school with a gun
on his hip. School just released for the day."

Did you see him?
               "No, I didn't. I'm in

the office."

"*What's your position with the School?*"

"I'm school secretary. I'm rather exposed right now." More questions. More squawking from the walkie-talkie. "*Announce Lockdown!*" "*Get everybody back inside the school!*" The reporting parent continued his blow by blow from the vestibule. "Now he's getting in a car. He's driving slowly down the street."

Who is he looking for? I repeat his words to the operator. She goes silent as she types, "*Bear with me a moment.*"

Four minutes and five seconds she kept me on the phone. Like a fool, I stood my ground in the middle of a glass enclosed office, exposed to anyone with desire to harm an easy target.

From announcing LOCKDOWN to declaring an ALL CLEAR took about three minutes. When I hung up from the operator I noticed a police officer in front of the school interviewing the parent who reported seeing a gun.

The call was longer than police travel time and the length of time it took to confirm the suspect had left the premises.
Question:
Why had she kept me on the phone so long?
It was troubling. I had told her I was exposed. She never told me police had arrived on site. Why not?

The expected proper Lockdown Signal
announcement is: *"Lockdown! Locks, Lights, Out of
Sight! Lockdown! Locks, Lights, Out of Sight! Your at-
tention please! This is Ms. Jones, school secre-
tary Ms. Jones. The situation has
been resolved and it's now safe to return
to normal activities."*
                             What I said
was: *"The situation has been resolved.
Please return to normal activities.
Get home safe."*

                 I was critiqued for not read-
ing the statement verbatim.

It was the third of three lockdowns in my
only semester at a neighborhood
school and my first gun threat announcement. Turned
out the reported parent owned a store
where he wears a gun. He had a concealed
carry license. He forgot to take it
off to pick-up his child from school. Police
gave him a warning. Never mind the gun
was fully visible on his hip while
on school grounds. Forget about the five to
ten minutes of terror he caused just by
going about his day, or the trauma
memory he added to so many
other dormant anxiety triggers.

Four shots!

Every time I almost die, I realize,
I'm not ready. July 27,
2024, approximately
10:53pm could have been my
time of death. The flash of gunfire in front
of my car on a pitch-dark street will be
forever emblazoned on my mind.

Are
there memories in death? Is there recall
of how we crossed over?
Who knows. I may
be dead already. Maybe I've long been
in hell envisioning different ways
of dying. Perhaps my mind is telling
me I'm no longer with the living. There's
no way to be sure. No one to tell. No
close people to hunt who could point to my
absence. There are no witnesses to my
life. No one left to speak upon my death.
I could be walking around in ghost form
in a hologram of my memory.
Thinking I'm still breathing – like I managed
to drive from four shots fired directly
at my windshield. I swear I thought I was
hit. I clutched my chest as a man landed on
my hood and something shattered against my
windshield. I don't know if anyone was
harmed. People had been partying in the
street. Now they were screaming, running, dropping
behind cars. I opened my door to duck
below the glass, to crawl out, but I was
still strapped in. Then I realized the car
was still moving forward.

God and a seat

belt kept me! My instinct was to get out
of the shooter's line of sight. God drove me
directly towards them. My rational
mind suggests I mistook firecrackers for
gunfire. But the sight that sees in the dark,
recognizes another demonic
attempt on my life. I didn't just dodge
four bullets. Four shots didn't just miss me.
I was guided through the fire and carried
to safety. Imagine the plans God has
for me that He so blatantly thwarted
the enemy with a *"Not her! Not now!"*
duck and drive maneuver. My senses say
I'm still alive.

> *... from his mouth the serpent*
> *poured water like a river after the*
> *woman, to sweep her away with the flood*
> *But the earth helped the woman; it opened*
> *its mouth and swallowed the dragon's river.*
> *Revelations 12:15-16*

Trauma of the Unseen

Many traumas ripple through a life.
Remembered, forgotten, long ago
feeling like now. How to tell
what's real or simply perception
from trauma tinted-lenses?
Impossible to know which reality
they exist in. Are the traumatized
even aware of their state?
One learns to revel in solitude.
Being alone seems the best
route to a trauma-free life.
Quietness, broken by occasional
conversations with strangers,
sometimes labeled as friends.
All while knowing, true friends don't
allow their friends to rot unseen.
Unheard. Unfelt. Unknown.

Too Tired for Anger

Anger drains energy.
It's exhausting.
Simply getting out of bed and
moving through a daily routine
requires the quiver full of
energy and care.

I'm too tired for anger.
Too exhausted to care
about grievances I can't remember
or don't want to fight about.

I'm pass forgiveness.
So over wanting to hear an apology
for heartbreaks that shattered
me into unrecognizable shards
shoved into the dark shadowy
corners of everyone's virtual space.

I'm so done with wanting to talk
about everything that has
made me a distant relative to myself
and a stranger to the world.

What does any of it matter?
How would apologies repair time?
Does forgiveness really revive relationships?
Will light flesh out the ghosts of loved ones?

I'm too tired to mourn.
I've lost so many it's hard to see
who's left. Lifting and moving dead weight
out of the way has blinded and numbed me.

> *Pray for the living...*
> *Pray for the dead...*

Pray for the living dead....
Pray for myself.
Pray for myself.

All I can do is pray for myself,
and those who have gone,
and those who remain.
May God bless us all
and keep us in His peace.

And do not grieve the Holy Spirit of God, by whom you were
sealed for the day of redemption. Let all bitterness and wrath
and anger and clamor and slander be put away from you,
along with all malice. Be kind to one another, tenderhearted,
forgiving one another, as God in Christ forgave you.
~ Ephesians 4:30-32

Remembering Gentleness

Today I mourn all the lost days –
all the lost time – hope bound me to.

Today I remember calling a man gentle.
Thinking that man was an outlier -
Different from all the harsh, aggressive men
I'd encountered throughout life.
I remember having a vision of him loving me
well, deeply, for a lifetime.
The possibility fueled hope for years,
until I could no longer justify his absence,
excuse his unwillingness to be mine.
Life has since proven my vision a lie.
My God! How did I hold on to it for so long?
Ironically, the thought of a gentle man
had me in a chokehold.

Are there any lovers of Black Women?
Why does our resilience signal the world
to handle us extra roughly?
Unfortunately, we too have historically
taken our cue from destroyers.
We weren't taught to be gentle
with ourselves or one another.
We stumble and struggle through life
toughening our skin, scrambling for a bit
of relief; learning to survive without help;
adapting to invisibility, disregard, and
being disappointed with the meager crumbs
slung our way in lieu of love, care,
tenderness, or consideration.
Expecting to live free of constant targeted
hateful acts intended to demoralize,
diminish, punish, and subjugate us
shouldn't be a losing proposition.

With our eyes we see how other women
are loved, honored, cared and provisioned for,
protected, supported, respected,
heard and seen when their strength fails them;
when they need community;
when their resources aren't enough;
when they can no longer cope.
If it's possible with them, it's possible to
remember gentleness with Black Women.

I hear the destroyers scoffing,
but for some reason, hope still has me
anticipating the day Gentleness
will cover my life and shame the world.

But now murderers!

But now murderers have forced
the world to bear witness to mass murder!
But now imperialists have forced
their citizens to finance mass genocides!
Ahhhh, now the Prince of the Air
has made us all complicit in the destruction
of our brothers, sisters, and children!
How can anyone possibly stand
when Judgment comes to the world?

We would not be complicit,
but how can we deny funding a government
that wage wars on defenseless people
around the world repeatedly?
Undercover, in shadows by proxy,
These sneaky death dealers have never
chosen life! They never offer truth.
They bind us to acts that will harm
many nations for generations and
weigh all our souls for eternity.

Arrogance of evil

The Israelites cried out to the Lord:
We have sinned against You,
forsaking our God and serving the Baals.
~ Judges 10:10

Promised Land
Fertile Crescent
Holy Land
What promises did God
give with the Land?

Milk, honey, abundance!
Multiplication of blessings.
Wherever His People go,
There HE IS.

Egypt
Sinai
Canaan
Philistia
Philistine
Palestine
Israel
Judah
Red Sea
Dead Sea
Mediterranean Sea

Again, Israel did evil in the eyes of the Lord
They did not turn away from the sins of their fathers.
~ Judges 10

Who did he promise it to?
Where are His Chosen?
Who said the Chosen were the Only?

Has God not chosen and chastised?
Rebuked? Rejected?
Admonished abominations?
Destroyed for do-overs?
When has God, the One Who IS,
Has Always BEEN and Will Always BE,
Allowed the Advocate of Destruction
Free reign without
Providing a way out
For those who love Him?
A triumphant return for those
Living according to His purpose?
When has He not provided
Comfort and recourse for those
Brutalized with savagery?

Evildoers today are no different than
their ancient predecessors. Their ruin will come.
Their pride and greed will meet justice.
The Lord warned Israel and Judah
Through all His prophets and seers:

> *"Turn from your evil ways. Observe my command*
> *and decrees, in accordance with the entire law that*
> *I commanded your ancestors to obey and that I delivered to*
> *you through my servants the prophets."*
> *~ 2 Kings 17:13*

God's Word Will Stand

He promised a nation
He promised to lead
His word performs for the obedient
For those who chase his heart
Adhere to His doctrine
Sit at His feet
Honor His Creation
Seek to understand
Those without blood on their hands
Those not prone to anger and distractions
Those who do not stray in their vows
Who perform wisdom and loyalty with discernment
God is faithful
He is fair
He's a Protector, Provider
He's an Architect, Planner & Builder
He knows the hearts of those who claim Him
and those who reject His presence
His edicts, His nature, His plans for the World
No one can destroy God's
Creation and claim to love Him
Beyond the end of the Earth
God's Word will Stand

Gentleness is an affront to brutality

The world is so full of brutal men,
brutality is the norm of the world.
Gentleness is ostracized.
Women across the globe prefer
to encounter bears in the wild
than men in "civilization."
In a world full of brutal men,
gentle men are an affront,
traitors to "the brotherhood."
While women are prey, hunted
ceaselessly by men.

Gentle men, much like women, don't
receive the respect or appreciation
their rareness so richly deserves.

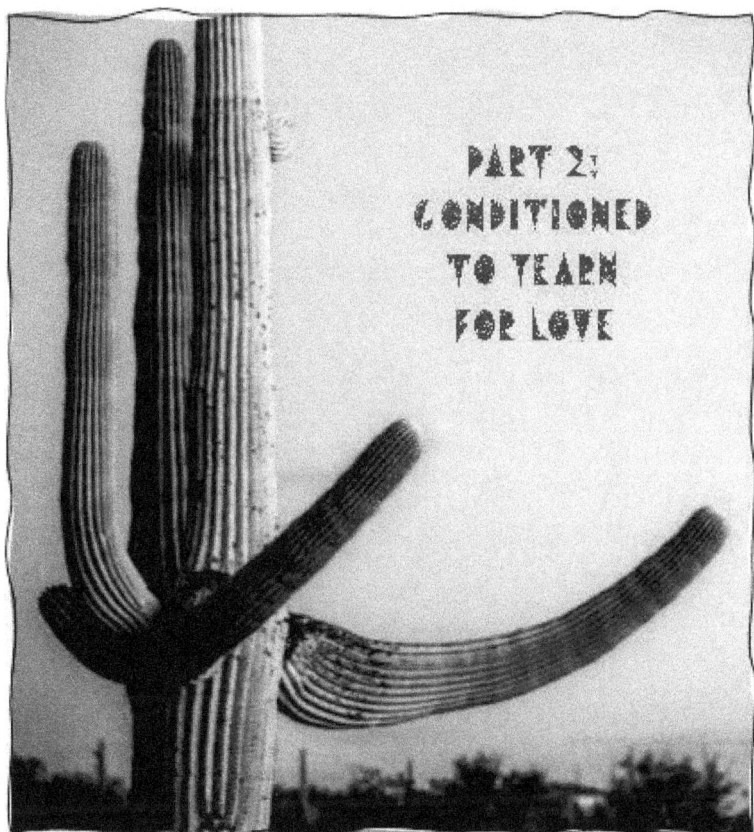

PART 2:
CONDITIONED
TO YEARN
FOR LOVE

Love is Labor

We cannot know how deep or resilient hope is until we experience its revival after a period of devastation. After experiencing the revival of my hope in my late thirties, it's not possible for me to be completely hopeless. However, my hope has become abstract in a murky darkness. There is no longer any detail in my visions and no fire in my passions. This is not a report claiming Love has failed - for that would be an impossible lie. I'm reporting that the people I have crossed paths with have not been interested in a love that looks like me, sounds like me, feels like me. I've been observing how people are not interested in sharing time or conversation with me. There are certainly those who are content to dump their trash into my ears and life, while refusing to share any measure of their joy with me. That doesn't benefit relational growth.

I thought my faith journey would only produce more love, joy, peace and wisdom.

The world teaches that love is a soft thing – warm, cuddly, tender, weak. Perhaps those who bask in the labor of someone else's love experience warmth and softness, but those who labor *to love*... well, we weather tempestuous storms, debilitating uncertainty and endure heart-breaking, on-the-job training. We don't immediately see the benefits of the humiliation, shame, loneliness, sadness, abuse or temptations that hammer at us throughout the workday. However, when we get to a certain point on our walk, we are able to look back and see where one humiliation prepared us for the next... until humiliation was no longer a concern. We see how shame shrouded us in darkness... until we decided to cast off the weight of shame and expose ourselves to more light. We can look back and see how loneliness felt excruciating for a time... but it was only in our aloneness that we were able to draw closer to God.

~ *"... and the people said, 'HELL NO!'"*
Desert of Solitude, 2020

Why is marriage a Woman's life goal?

A question from the Twitter-verse: Why is
marriage a woman's life goal? Better to
ask, "Why are women only counted as
wives and mothers?" The answer to both is:
Conditioning and indoctrination.
In society, marriage and mother-
hood are the highest goals, purpose, and best
achievement of every girl's life. Nothing
else is taught or lauded, supported or
respected. Men marry "girls" who are taught
that being chosen by a man is the
beginning of life. Since we all want to
live "good lives" we dream what we are trained to
dream: of being chosen to become a
wife and mother. Only then does girlhood
morph into adulthood. Man's seed transforms
the adult *girl* into a mother. At
no point, is a woman honored as she
is on her own, by herself. She's only
acknowledged for who she is to others:
daughter, sister, friend, wife, mother, worker,
supporter, helper, caretaker. What if
all she wants is to be who she is to
herself? A Woman. Intentionally
formed. Created to have her own lived goals,
plans, experiences, and life story.

Conditioning and indoctrination
being what they are, how does a Woman
on her own live without yearning for all
she doesn't have and may no longer want?

A Cry

Was this the life
You originally planned
for me? Or did I mess up?
Did I miss the mark?
Ignore an opportunity?
What did I do?
Or not do?
Mercy. Please. Mercy.
This can't be all there is!

Emptiness follows

Emptiness doesn't stay behind
no matter how it's filled,
replaced, changed,
shaken, disrupted
reimagined
ignored
emptiness is empty,
voraciously hungry,
untenable, deeply unfillable
void
barren
dark
sad
listless
but somehow, it's not useless
the unquenchable nature
of emptiness leads to
yearning
striving
a ceaseless
pursuit of joy and
all good things
which can only
route to peace
eventually

Life is Happening

So many years
wasted
waiting
wanting
forgetting
life is always happening
it doesn't accommodate our schedule
or ask for an appointment
it isn't scouting for the perfect environment
or adjusting for the most flattering angle
it doesn't care about having
enough money, enough time
enough energy or enough of anything
life is simply happening
it's on-going and going on
don't let it pass you by
don't get left behind
while looking back
or too far ahead
be where you are – fully
life is happening there today
whatever you're doing
wherever you have your being
life does as it does
it continues to happen
whether you're ready or not
it will happen no matter what
don't waste it on hopes for tomorrow
don't wait to live out loud
don't allow your wants
to diminish what you have
forget what isn't
relish what is
honor who you are now

Midnight train to East Harlem

Night Crawler is me
Exiting the house after 6 pm
Looking for something to do
A place to be
Two hours in
One event down
What else to do
Where else to go
Anyplace but
Home alone
The city that never sleeps
Always seems to remind me
I sleep and live alone
Every night and day

♫# *In the jungle, the mighty jungle*
The lion sleeps tonight... ♭ ♫
But not this lioness
Last movie of the night
"Sorry to Bother You"
Was a bother to get to
And stay awake for
Walking through the
East Village to the 6 train
Felt like a stroll along
A desolate road
Sitting on a train full of
Empty looking commuters
Finally provided
Some comfort in going home

Nothing I Want Here
Thoughts upon leaving New York City

There's nothing I want here
No more dreams to chase
Idols to praise
Goals to reach
Empires to build

I arrived with a vision
A drive, boundless energy
Passion and determination
Irrepressible idealism
And a plan to achieve success
In less than five years

All I needed was access
An audience
Readers
Supporters
Reviewers

Lack of money would not be
My downfall
Being on my own
Would not deter me
Investing all my hard earned
Income to bring the vision to fruition
Was not a problem
The dream is
Self-funded
Self-made
Accountable to no one
But God
My creativity
My choice
My success
My failure
My definition

The lights remain as
Bright as the first day
They dazzled me
Though still beautiful
I no longer see
Magic, glitter or hope
I see artifice and greed
These lights are not for
Sight or guidance
They are distraction
Leading to a multitude
Of sins
What's your pleasure
What's your vice
Your secrets will flourish here
Your pain will multiply
Your darkness will grow to consume you
If you aren't careful.
If you aren't able to see through
The artificial light
Don't be blinded
Don't be fooled
All is folly in New York City

What is a friend?

What is a friend if not someone
who shows up to share their presence
as they participate in your life?
Someone who may join in your daily activities,
special milestones, or simply sit with you in silence.
What is a friend, if not someone who opens
their life to you, reciprocating a cycle
of care and support to deepen the relationship?
If there isn't such a "someone" in your life,
can anyone truly claim to be your friend?

If, when departing

It's time to go!
Get up! Get out! Get moving!
But where to? What now?
How to welcome what's next?

If when departing
A place –
a job, a home, a city –
You feel joy unspeakable
Then that was not your place.
It was not for you.
If when departing a space,
you know you will
miss nothing and no one
left behind, then you are not
leaving community or home.
You are a stranger leaving strangers,
people who refused to welcome you.

Don't despair! Shake them off!
Move on. Continue your journey.
Enjoy what you can. Embrace moments.
Cultivate hope. *Build your place within*.
Carry it with you.

Eventually, perhaps, just maybe
you will find community in people who
welcome you as you are,
nourish you as you grow,
and bless your spirit as you
move about the world.

lessons from solitude

being alone doesn't always equal lonely
company rarely equals companionship
solitude needs to be protected
as do you and your space
someone who can sit quietly
with a solitary person is a rare find
inviting others into your peace often taints it
invitations must be withdrawn
when the invited become unwelcome
open doors require filters
but the strongest aid to reclaim
a tranquil home is a closed door
relaxing and rebalancing can be daily activities
wherever you are becomes your home
home becomes the sanctuary
where you grow into the sacredness
of your own presence and peace

Billions and billions of possibilities

Oh, the lies I've chosen
to tell myself!
Painful to think about
considering hopes, dreams
fantasies and ambitions.
Living in a mental wonderland –
is it protection, self-preservation
or a whole alternate universe?
Perhaps in some dimension I am happy,
loved, held and honored.
Somewhere in the billions and
billions of created possibilities,
I've surely been wanted for who I am –
a whole human with human needs?
Hopefully, somewhere, at some point.
But not here, not now.
Not by anyone I've held
in high, tender regard.
What a tragic waste
life seems to be.

Life without love

Without love, there is no suffering,
but what is life without love?
If pain is love's tax,
then growth must be a reward.
All hurts will pass
but their lessons remain.

I only ever wanted to love

I've only ever wanted
to feel love
to see it, hear it,
be touched by it.
Embraced
Held
Sheltered
Protected
Covered in love.

I've only ever wanted
for love to have an overflowing
presence in my life.
To function as a mantle,
a spiritual veil,
an emotional cover,
a psychological barrier
against all the barbarism in the world,
all the terror in this realm.
Against the banal brutality so prevalent
in so many spaces and places.

I've only ever wanted Love
to be what it claims to be;
filling and flowing through me
to saturate relationships
environments, daily life.
Instead, like an illusion,
a dangling carrot, a hammer,
Love has become a suggestion,
a vague point of reference
an impossible life goal
used as a controlling agent by people
with no concept of what Love is.

Ecclesiastes

nothing matters
all is in vain
try hard
or don't try at all
we all meet the same end
whatever our choices
no matter our inaction
despite our protests
no matter our thoughts
life presses on
stress overwhelms
joy becomes illusive
fear persists
anxiety grows
heartache
bleeds us dry

If, in leaving a place...

If, in leaving a place,
those you leave behind
sigh in relief and give thanks to
God for your departure,
you can trust you offered no good
provided nothing of substance,
added no value
to the space you vacated.

If, in leaving a place,
your absence
brings relief and praise
then your presence must
lean towards darkness.
Hate, malice, venom are choices.
You chose to do wrong.
Plotted to go out of your way
to cause harm. You speak death even as
you're wrapped in the embrace of life.
I have no sympathy for your wayward travels.
I spoke caution for the danger
you're rushing towards
offered respite from the
consequences of your choices.
Warm shelter and a full belly
in the midst of a concrete jungle.
You took what you wanted
wasted the remainder unnecessarily.
Misused, overused and abused my hospitality.
You left with no appreciation of the
safe harbor you cast aside in
favor of lies and misrepresentations.
You have no understanding of grace.
Said not one "*thank you*"
Showed no gratitude
Didn't even leave a: ♪♯*Dear John, by the time*

you read this line, I'll be gone... ♭ ♫
No, instead you left a petition
for an order of protection
claiming harassment and abuse.
As if I were the one who
showed up on your doorstep
without warning or invitation.
You filed for a restraining order
as if I were the one sleeping in your
home with ill intent, plotting
against your peace
dreaming of your downfall.
There are no squatter's rights
in an occupied home. Just leave.

Entitled complaints all.
As if you have a right
to my life, my property, my income,
my provision, my inheritance
simply because you showed up
and lusted for the fruit of my
praise, hard work and perseverance.
My struggle. My survival.
I have no curses to hurl at you.
There's no need.
You aren't worth my frustration.
When I opened my home to you,
I made available to you everything
God has made available to me.
You have no idea how blessed you were
sitting in the shelter of the grace that covers me.
You rejected that when you attacked me.

A character like yours
doesn't require strong sight to see.
Your stench permeates around you.
It turns the edges of the space you inhabit.
You are your own worst enemy,
but you think you're a boss,

making boss moves.
Penthouse self-aggrandizement
in a borrowed *Top Ramen* reality.
  Check yourself.
  Check yourself.
  Check yourself,
  'Cause you're
  Wr-wr-wr-wreckin' yourself.

If, in leaving a place,
those you leave behind
are filled with satisfaction and joy,
then your "boss move" –
your departure –
was actually an
answered prayer.

Thank you for testing
my faith and resolve.
Thank you for dropping in.
Thank you so much more for leaving!

Finally, be strong in the Lord and in the strength of
his power. Put on the whole armor of God, so that
you may be able to stand against the wiles of the
devil. For our struggle is not against enemies of
blood and flesh, but against the rulers, against the
authorities, against the cosmic powers of this
present darkness, against the spiritual forces of
evil in the heavenly places.
~ Ephesians 6:10-12

Why am I out here struggling?

Why am I out here struggling as if New York City
won't welcome me back? Embrace me fully,
enrich and enlighten me, incite and excite me.
Embrace and support me while
keeping me well fed and hydrated.

Why am I out here paying New York City prices
for no New York City stimulation, access or benefits?
Amenities, opportunities, diversity or flavor?
What good are cities I can't walk around
to see people peopling. hear sounds sounding,
smell smells smelling? Can't get flavors, textures,
colors, ideas, conversations or inspiration?
Why miss out on a whole world of diverse dimensions
accessible with a simple walk to the subway,
office cafeteria, or the mailbox in the lobby?

How is it possible to pay more for food in
Tucson and Milwaukee, than New York?
How does *Five Guys* charge more
in the desert than in Penn Station?
How do restaurants a short drive from
Mexico's border make guacamole with no kick?
Everything's bland, quaint, uninspiring.
It's all far too expensive for where it is.
Nothing excites my palate. Nothing encourages
an extended stay. I could leave it all today
and remember none of it tonight.

Why am I out here struggling in a favorless food
desert? In a bland, pitiful, ridiculous dearth of taste,
when there's New York City to return to?

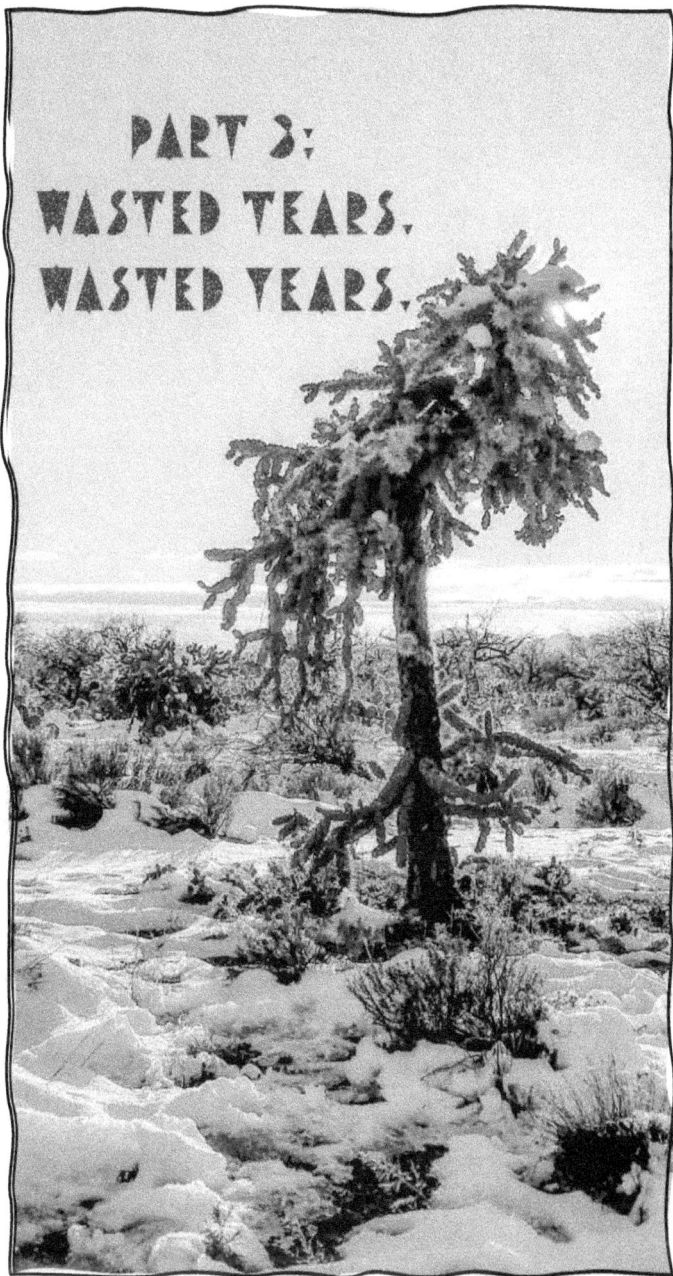

PART 3:
WASTED TEARS,
WASTED YEARS.

Everything is Love

People in the world will mess you up. It took a great deal of time, effort and concentration for me to focus on God's character defining love. I had to let go of, and forget, the treatment I had received from people who said they loved me but never actually showed me love. Because of their way of expressing "love," I found it hard to trust and surrender to God when I first embarked on my spiritual journey – my life walk with my Creator. I had to purge what I knew of the world, and act in faith according to what I believed in the Spirit. Then I had to become open to the full cycle of giving and receiving.

Years ago, I heard a quote: *"Everything is love; hurt and anger only try to mask it."* It's not really possible to hide love. That quote got me through a lot of hurt and many stages of anger. Eventually, I developed the ability to express myself fully, which made me more receptive to other people's self-expression. I stopped running from expressions of anger and stayed around to try to resolve issues. I stopped avoiding hurt and faced it, often attempting to soothe it.

Don't you want to show yourself clearly and be known fully by someone? With no fear of recrimination, rejection or judgment? This is the best way to boldly reveal yourself and accept others in their true state as well. When you remove the reason for hiding, fear has no opportunity to dig roots into you.

~ *"Show Me the Love"*
The Process of Asking for, Receiving
and Giving Love & Forgiveness, 2012

The Dream

In my dream state he said,

"I want to be where you are."

My heart whispered back,

"Then come, my love, be with me."

He is my sweetness.

He is my sweetness.
When we aren't right,
he's also the source of
all my bitterness.

Lover of my soul

Man, my soul loves,
I always want to see you.
Even when I don't
want to be bothered,
your presence refreshes me,
revives me, sends currents
through this long dormant body.
Seeing you...
oh, to see you
is to know,
I, too, am seen.

His smile is everything

His smile is everything.
Or perhaps, everything
is in his smile.
Other women get excited
over pecs, abs,
money, cars,
dinner, nice clothes.
They squeal over passing photos
the likelihood of having a
man-toy for a night,
for a fling,
for whatever needs arise.
Short term, steady, with or
without a ring.
But I swear,
nothing grips my heart like
his smile –
shy, engaging,
full, amazing,
wide and welcoming.
His smile is everything –
breath, life, hope.
It carries a glimmer of admiration,
beginning of forever,
end of rejection,
bloom of acceptance,
belonging, safe harbor,
possibility of home.

Thoughts on Touching

Imagining feeling a touch
Is an aphrodisiac
A firm guiding hand on my upper arm
A bristled cheek against mine
A well-furred thigh rubbing along
the smoothness of my dimpled thighs
The touch of textured skin
The thought of experiencing
A Man, *MY Man*
Dancing the mating tango of flesh
With the mambo of breath mingling
His *cha cha* to my *sashay*
As we lay, roll, arch, thrust
Drumbeats
Heart throbs
Pulsating nerves
Erupting veins
Excited explosions
Simply at the thought
Of being touched

I just wanna

I just wanna make love to you.
That's it
That's all
No fuss
Perhaps a whole lot of mess
Rocking
Rolling
Soothing
Sucking
Joy. Joy. Joy.

I just wanna find my joy in you
That's it
That's all
No complications
Just a whole lot of laughter
Openness
Deepness
Sharing
Caring
Smile. Smile. Smile.

I just wanna smile again with you
That's it
That's all
No guile or hiding
Just a whole bunch of carefree
Deep-rooted
Nerve-tingling
Goose-pimpling
Stomach-quivering
Love. Love. Love.

You Know

You know
Where I want you
Here deep close
You know
How I want you
Every way completely
You know
When I want you
Now today all tomorrows

Sleeping in

Upon waking in my warm,
spacious bed, my hands survey
my body. Gliding, gripping, cupping,
squeezing breasts, belly, hips, thighs,
trailing dips, rolling on mounds
shifting to my side, I trace myself
from another angle.
Admiring gravity's work on
the fullness God blessed me with.
Thick waist, bountiful belly,
broad hips framing still-high buttocks,
long tapered thighs with quads
too tight to be healthy muscle.

Gazing into the distance,
I imagine waking with a partner,
my husband, a man devoted to
exploring all my secret spaces,
awakening me to all the
unseen and unimagined joys
locked within my body.
His firm hand and a tender touch
burns a light trail across my skin
branding me with each caress,
he claims me every time
he pulls me close.
All I can do is cling,
eager to cleave, inhale
his scent, drown in his sultry eyes,
taste his skin as I chase sensations.
Rock to the sound of his voice
coursing along my skin,
playing tunes on standing hairs.
Enjoy his textures, flavor, firmness.

Smiling at the thought
of his fullness joining mine
so completely as he fills more
than the empty space next to me
in the soft glow of early morning.

Yes, please.
(aka Horny for the Holidays)

Are we doing this?
Yes, please.
Bring your lips to mine.
Yes, please.
Pull my hips to yours.
Yes, please.
Nibble the curve of my neck
Yes, please.
Suckle the bounty of my breasts
Yes, please.
Lick and tease my button of joy
Yes, please.
Can I climb you now?
Yes, please.
Explore the column of your neck
Yes, please.
Slide across the expanse of your chest
Yes, please.
Glide with your righteous joy bringer
Yes, please.
I want to cradle you where you fit best
Yes, please.
In my arms
Between my thighs
Enshrined in my temple
Merged heart to heart
Massaging my mind
Yes, please.

Surrender

Okay. I yield.
Call. I'll answer.
Show up. I will open.

I Will

I will love every part of you
Even as I hate the thought
Of you creating life outside of me

Superpower

He thinks his superpower
is his handsomeness.
Beautiful though he is,
his gentleness was my kryptonite
until his cavalier dismissiveness
left callouses on my heart.

He was a super man
when his strength represented
shelter for my vulnerability.
I would've given anything to explore
the known and unknown universe in his arms.
Holding him as he held me.
I would have sacrificed
my selfishness to be his
Fortress of Solitude,
nurturing him even as he fed me.

Though I prayed for a man
who stands strong in his power,
I truly need one who revels
in wielding his gentleness; who
understands the graceful
power of tenderness.

Everything I've asked for in a partner,
I've worked to be a match for.
Love is my fortifying mantle,
Compassion a laser focus.
His short-sightedness
didn't allow any hope for us.
My disappointment paved the way
to my spinster origin story:

> *She who sought love from another*
> *found true love within herself.*

I can't do this for you.

I can't do this for you.
You have an opening,
It's for you to walk through.
You have a need.
It's for you to accept fulfillment
Acknowledge your error
Your loss
Your sorrow
And remorse
Release it all.
Embrace correction, forgiveness.
Your reward
Your heart
Your joy
Embrace it all.
I want you to win.
I want you to get over yourself.
I'm on the over side,
Been waiting a long time
To win with you.

About control

If you want to control me,
please me. So simple.
Contributing no pleasure to my life –
mind, body, soul, spirit –
affords you no satisfaction.

See me.
Hear me.
Touch me.
Be present with me.
Engage me with intention, purpose.
pure spirit and upright character.
Seek me openly with
vulnerability and truthfulness.
Receive me with the same.
Manifest your will with words –
speak your mind
express your hopes
reveal your plans.
I need to hear your voice;
dwell with your spirit.

What vision drives you?
What goals are you chasing?
Share yourself so I can
meet you where you are.
How do you see us?
How do you value me?
I'll grant some control in a partnership,
but if being with me is only about
your wants, your needs, your plans, your life,
then we'll both be deeply disappointed.
No control for you.
No pleasure for me.

Use your words

You're going to have to use words
spoken from your mouth to my ears.
Truth my heart can discern.
Speak, listen, share,
also known as
conversation,
heart to heart,
roadmap to
whatever's to come.
State intent,
ask, answer, declare
who you are,
who you want to be,
who you choose to be
to me, for me, with me.
I need words. Direct. Clear.
Unambiguously your voice.
This is grace.

I want to be able to
recall your words,
hold you to what you say –
experience their manifestation
as an inevitable outcome.
Allow me to take you at your word,
see you in your word,
trust your intentions,
and respond accordingly.

Simple Impossible

Never asked you
to outperform
anyone or anything.
Only wanted
to know you,
join you,
grow with you.
Exchange loving care,
as life partners
How did so simple
become so impossible?

Why are you so different?

Why is it so hard to forgive the hurt you give?
The lonely sadness you make?
The insecurities you create?
You're not the only one
intent on making me miserable.
So many have tried. They all failed.
Caring not how they hated me,
I shook them off. Kept walking,
continued growing, embraced
spiritual evolution. I became more
even as they strove to diminish me.

But you... only you
have succeeded in pausing my life.
You lassoed my heart
with a rope that burns into
every fiber of my being.
I keep berating myself for
not letting you go, but
truth is I'm angry you
refuse to release me.
Keeping me enslaved to memory,
hope, a distant vague promise of us.
While never loving me,
never speaking to me
never touching me.
Abdicating joy, abstaining
from life with every breath.

Why are you so different from others?
Why can't I shrug away your rejection?
Unfortunately, there's no other I want to love,
touch, or share my life's breath with.
For these reasons, it's hard to
forgive you for not wanting me.

modern no-mance

black man don't wanna be black
intrigued by a black woman who wants him
chooses to gaslight and shame her
for daring to see him as a possible partner

Attention Seeker

You have my attention
never lost it, despite
trampling it with dismissive ridicule.
What will you do with it now?
What have you ever done
to keep my focus and hope
other than laugh and brag with friends
while keeping me in perpetual limbo?
Indeed, have you ever given me
your purposeful attention?
Directed your energy on me?
Strove to be more than
a *nice guy* liked by everyone?
Did you ever envision yourself
as a man of integrity standing by my side?
A man of purpose joining your strength to my vision?
Unlikely, as your form of noncommunication,
layered with emotional hiding
seduced me into the shadows.

I can think all the thoughts
or none at all, do nothing, say nothing
and get the same wide-eyed,
"I'm a nice guy!" non-response
received when I did everything
to look like a fool out of my depth.

> *A foolish woman, who gathered*
> *all her available courage*
> *to speak all her known words*
> *of admiration, love and desire*
> *to a being who sparked the light*
> *in her spirit yet could not comprehend*
> *the nature of her offer.*

It took years to appreciate my vibration

was beyond your frequency.
You couldn't perceive me beyond
the physical appearance you considered
unworthy of your commitment.
My attention meant nothing
when it was all I had to give,
even though it's what you wanted
most from me. Attracted to my
light with no respect for it.
Still, here we are circling one another.
Before I put weight to cryptic social
media nudges, what are your intentions?
Do I willingly enter your rabbit hole of
emotional grief, with no hope of any satiation,
to allow you to feast off my energy?
Watch you eat, as I starve?
Dote on your basking, as I wither?
Admire you soaring, as I drown?

You chose someone else.
I grew in grace, seeking understanding
from a God who would put you
in my spirit yet keep you out of my life.
Maybe you were never *"The One"*
I was to commit my future to.
Perhaps, the real test is trusting God
to provide beyond what I perceive
in a life set on orbiting you.

Fuck Mr. Nice Guy

I need a man
A stand up man
With a kind heart
Revolutionary mind
A man unconcerned with
pleasing the world
But focused on pleasing me
Nice does nothing
Kind changes environments
Relationships
Culture

Kindness is love in action
Niceness is projected imagery
Smoke and mirrors
To sell likeability
Popularity
Availability
It's a falseness
Who are you truly available for?
What you stand for
determines where you fall.

Well-liked by all.
Deeply loved by none.

No Straight Lines

If life isn't linear,
then we've already loved,
believing years wasted away
waiting for what's
already been.

If love isn't chronological,
surely there are no regrets.
Deja vu confirms
what's come and gone.
Past is prologue to future's past.
Reality is never knowing you
even as my spirit calls you home.
Though we've only shared
shy fleeting touches, my body
flushes with memory of joys
yet to come. How can
there be certainty of tomorrow
while languishing on yesterday's
dead-end paths?

If life were a straight line,
perhaps we would have missed
each other in the rush to reach
all the next destinations.
Perhaps, it's better that we met on
this long, winding road and
continued our separate paths.
Perhaps, combusting too early
would've been mutual destruction.
Fire that once consumed may
now only keep us warm.
Comfortable enough to sustain life,
not enough current to turn back time.
Maybe we needed to learn to control

passions, hopes, expectations.
Maybe we needed to unlearn
biases, roles, assumptions.
Is that reductive reasoning?
A function of call and response?

If existence is a squiggly
fifth dimensional experience,
suffering must be an element
necessary for elevating consciousness.
I see you. I feel you.
Yet you're always out of reach;
present in mind, absent in body.
Still, I'm here. Where,
in the continuum, are you?
How do we reconcile space, time, and
waiting through choices that made
parted ways divergent lives?

this is a test

this is a test
and only a test

if I do nothing
what happens?
if you do nothing
what happens?
if I do something
or anything
perhaps one more thing
what happens?
if you do nothing still
what happens?
if I do everything
all things
reach down, move your feet
or up to puppet your lips
what happens?
and if at the end of it all
you still do nothing
what could have
possibly happened?

your heart and will
are yours to control.
mine are mine to protect.

for every level of effort
I perform,
the outcome remains
no forward motion
no synchronicity
no reciprocity
you taught me
do nothing
like you ....

flirt with the air
deny responsibility
through inaction
save energy
stay where I am
move forward
on my own momentum
with no expectations or
disappointments, after all,
we were only a test

no words

what can i say
how can i speak
i gave you all the words
i wished to live
only to watch them die
from your carelessness
i have nothing to say
other than
what's been spoken
nothing to give
other than
what's been offered
you seem to want
more than i have
other than who i am
someone not me
what can i say to that
other than
you once took my breath away
and i didn't mind
each gasp for air meant
you were near
for your closeness i
willingly traded my breath
until you took it as your tribute
and turned away
walked away
stayed away
how can i speak when
you never returned
never acknowledged
my sacrifice
you held me suspended
kept me choked
in an inattentive grip
weakening my gift

day by day
slowly killing me
painfully destroying
all i had to offer
yet you expect to revive me
simply by loosening your grip
from a distance
how can you breathe life
into me from a distance

Message in a Cyber Bottle

If you want to remain
in my head, so be it.
Who am I to ask you to evolve
beyond a fantasy
or suggestion?
To be present in the flesh
and not just a cyber distraction?
A hoax, an act,
generative AI, a composite
of thoughts, hopes, dreams,
a figment of my imagination
where false positives present
as double negatives?
Confirmation bias is still a lie;
I won't trust the screen
if I can't touch your face.

You follow me,
Watch me,
Mimic me,
Taunt me.
You show me all the ways
you can do without me
while signaling
"Help me!"
.   "Stop me!"
"Save me from myself!"
I'm neither savior nor enforcer.
I'm not here to persuade you
to be the man I thought
I saw in you a lifetime ago.
The man I wanted to share
my life and talents with
The man whose seed I wanted to
receive, nourish and grow in my womb.
Potential founders of generations together

reduced to someone the other used to know.

Certainty is confirmed with action.
I'm sorry I was so sure
when you were so far from ready.
It pains me to be unsure now
when you finally show signs of
embracing the vision.
Your resistance has been damaging,
not only to our time,
but to my understanding of everything.
What is love?
What is joy?
What benefits are faith and hope?
The dreams I dreamed,
the visions I saw, didn't prepare
me for decades of unrequited longing,
of intolerable aloneness,
of a deep sense of not being enough
or wanted enough to be pursued with
passion, love, purpose, intensity.

I was convinced you knew I am everything
God prepared me to be for you –
your suitable partner, blessing and comfort.
The One you till for, to keep and to cover,
to love as you love your own body.
Your resistance and withdrawal
shattered my conviction.
My understanding of relationships
warped. What is this cord?
How are our journeys parallel
without coordination?
How can I sense you so deeply
When I don't know you at all?
What is knowing?

Your voice is unique to my ears.
From the moment you first spoke

to me, I heard you as Shepherd –
a trusted voice I could listen to
without barriers. In all the ways
you communicate, I hear you.
Stunning how you breach the
vacuum of space separating us.

Do you remember when I told you
"My ears will always be open to you?"
The moment I typed those words
I knew an eternal truth, now proven,
despite the noise of life,
the messiness of your distractions,
my own attempts to deafen myself to you.
when everything seems meaningless,
you are the spark that animates my life,
making breathing worthwhile –
hope itself becomes joy.
A word from you and everything has meaning
I didn't make us this way
The *how's* and *whys* are as mysterious
to me as they may be to you.
Perfection was never a thought, but
assured consecration was understood.

Fallow Earth

Give me something
To go on
A word to hold on to
Love to lean into
Give me something to
Look forward to
A life to grow into
Seeds need more than dirt
They need air, sun, water
A gentle word and a helping hand
Create wonders
We are each gardeners
Of the soil we're planted in
Cultivators of relationships
We merge with
Weeding, grafting, replanting
All work
Your labor is required
Blooms reward effort
The harvest will be abundant
Planting, reaping, sowing
Watering one seed
May produce sustenance
For a thousand years
Aren't you tired of being hungry?
Isn't your mind weary of imagining?
How are your yearnings better than my flesh?
A bounty I carried, a bounty now fallow
Because you refuse to
Give me something, anything.
Give me everything. all of you.

What you wanna do?

If you truly want what you want
Get up and come get it
Subliminal messaging won't
Move you closer to touching,
caressing or holding me
Unfetter yourself
Reach out, ask, receive,
speak us into existence
Come close
Do what you wanna do
So I can be fully who I am
A blessing and a comfort
Beyond dreams and satisfaction
As you linger in the background

Answer me this:
Is we or is we ain't?
You got this?
or do I have to come get you?
If I get you
Then, who got me?
Do what you want as long as
you cover and keep me
Build and cultivate relationship
Grant the joy of proximity
The grace of shared presence
until there's no doubt
Of who WE is
    You are me
    I am you
    Together we are One
    One breath
    One thought
    One heart
    One spirit
    One body

One life

So, what you gonna do?
Stay motionless or move forward
You, me or we? All in for everything
or stay back for nothing but the status quo?

Help me help you help us

Help me help us:
Afraid of what?
Have you explored this
fear that has held you hostage
for a lifetime?
What did you have to lose by being
open, honest, communicative
that you haven't lost by being
dismissive, untrue, noncommittal?
What lies have you believed
acted on, performed wholeheartedly?
What's different now?
What has your fear morphed into
or has it dissipated?
Has your ever-imminent eruption happened
did it fizzle out?
Or have you learned to confront,
explore and manage the emotions
you were so afraid of sharing?

"Read between the lines," you say
while not honoring any of
my explicit words. How are you
still communicating
in code behind a screen?
How is this fulfilling for you?
Or are my expectations
for face-to-face, voice-to-voice
communication too elitist,
discriminatory or non-inclusive
for all communication types?
After all, if it's only about
sending, receiving, understanding,
responding, then effective
communication has been achieved.
Then again, how effective can

communication be when there's
no action behind it? What does
it matter if I hear and understand
the sense of what you type
but don't trust the message
is mine to receive? How do I know
you're not speaking to one
or a hundred other women?
Littering your communiqué with
words from your interactions with them?

When did I become
so difficult to speak with directly?
How do you not know your voice
opens me, moves me, pulls me in,
soothes me? Words from your
mouth to my ears are the key
to everything you need.
A step towards unbarricading the door
to my heart and spirit.
How do you not know you have
to move from behind the screen
with intention and purpose?
Trust yourself enough
to start moving in the direction
you desire to go. Give me an
opportunity to trust your actions.

Believe Him

When a man shows you
Repeatedly
He prefers the company of men
To your presence
Believe him
His smile is brighter with his buddies,
his pals, his friends
Spending time with them is his priority
His body language is open and relaxed
with them; closed and distant with you
Read the message as
Given
No benefit of the doubt
No mental gymnastics
No excuses
   He's shy
   He's unsure
   He's scared
   He doesn't want what he wants
   He's not ready to commit
Hogwash! All of it.
He knows he doesn't want a partnership *with you!*
He knows he doesn't want to honor you.
He knows he has no respect for you.
That's enough for you to let go.
Release yourself of hope;
free yourself of him.
Leave him to his fuckbuddies.
It has nothing to do with you.
Your willingness to turn into a pretzel
Won't make him a reciprocating mate.

If he doesn't want to make you his business –
his priority and focus – make sure he remains
none of yours. Know with certainty,

it's not you, it never was.
It's most definitely him.
Don't project potential
onto his hostile treatment.
Don't assume good intentions
or an eventual willingness to please you.
If a moment is enough to see a lifetime,
your life needn't be stunted
for one who has no moments for you.

Let go.
Move forward.
Breathe.
Release more.
Keep moving.
Breathe deeper.
Exhale fully.
Empty yourself.
Cleanse. Inhale deeply.
Live in your own joy.
Continue breathing, releasing.
You are everything you need.

I don't know what to say

Words once flowed freely from me,
without shame or embarrassment,
even when I goofed.

I thought there was a knowing,
an understanding,
a kinship beyond time and space.
A level of ease beyond
the comfort of our beginning.
All I needed to know about us –
who we would be to one another –
was imparted to me
when our hands first touched.

Sensing a future is not the same
as surviving until it unfolds.
If I had known decades would pass
between our first earnest handshake
and me being able to hold you
in my arms without letting go,
I would have doubted much sooner –
fallen to the wayside in despair,
or seduced you for a full sensory
memory to re-experience on demand.

No longer listening

I once heard what I thought
was a calling. A mating
call of yearning, of need,
of matched desire.
I listened.

Was someone seeking me?
The voice seemed familiar –
its vibration pierced my soul,
breached the dark midnight of my days
in the directionless wilderness of life.
It pulled me, spun me
surrounded and filled me.
The melody delighted me.
Surely it was a call to life;
to fulfill hopes and dreams.
I kept listening.

Even as I called back,
I listened.
Even after I became a seeker,
starving through the ravenous desire
of a supernova devouring its own light,
I listened.
I called back.
I listened.
I called back.
I waited and waited and waited.
For more than a dozen years,
I waited for my radiant reply to reach
the one my soul loved;
aching for the brilliance of his
presence to sustain me.

I thought I *needed* to see, feel,
be seen, heard, needed, wanted,

loved by someone I could love in return.
Yet aging with none no presumed needs met
altered my hearing, diminished my longing.
Silence is not only deafening,
it deadens the soul and mutes the heart.
I've stopped listening to the void.

A lifetime ago, a whisper tickled my senses
In the wilderness of the universe.
How could that be when
sound can't travel in space?
Relics of my imagination launched
on gases of hope, created spiraling galaxies
of dreams in the echo chamber of my heart.
What was there to hear other than silence?

Realizing the phantom sounds heard
in the wilderness of loneliness were
my own echoes reverberating off stardust,
recentered me. New focus: be all I can be
to myself. Feel, expand, keep moving.
My life needs me here, now.

Everything or Nothing

It wasn't enough to be
everything.
You wanted to be
nothing.
So be it.

When I Think About

When I think about

How I loved

I mean

How I wanted to love

Each time

I tried to love

Or rather how

The love I offered

Was always rejected

When I think about

Love In this world

My heart breaks

All over again

Love. A Postmortem

I once loved
With a purity of
Hope
Before
My love was tested
For conditions
By one who
Sought to break me
Now I love with an
Expectation
To be hurt
He meant me no good
So, he presented no
Goodness to me

Interesting
I didn't see that when
I saw us

This is why the world has
A shortage of Lovers
Those who love openly
Are hated viciously
By those they bare their
Hearts to
And each time the Lovers
Choose to love again
They are aware
Their love is poured from a
Tainted and ruptured vessel
From which it takes
Longer to give
And is harder to receive
This less pure
More defined
Conditional love

Hopes for little and
Expects the worse
The Lovers become less willing
To love those who don't
Love them. And that's how the
Lovers disappear from the earth

Forgotten

I am forgotten.

Therefore, I have

stopped remembering.

And just like that

And just like that
I'm left high and dry
again
set up to hope for a fantasy
led to believe out of billions and
billions of possibilities
you were turning fully to me
coming to declare yourself
finally
ready to claim and secure
the heart laid at your feet
decades ago
instead, you smiled... or rather
posted a smiling selfie
as if that was enough
to sustain all I've been holding on for
no surprise, though it still stings
no effort
no substance
no words
to validate all the turmoil
your irreverent peacocking
stirs up
repeatedly
tossing me and my message of wonder
back into the sea of silence

PART 4: RELEARNING WE

What is a Strong Black Woman?

He said he wanted to give me my flowers. He admired my strength as a strong Black Woman. He was proud to call me a friend.

My skeptical take-away is, *"What is a strong Black Woman?"*

Is she a woman forced to fend for herself? A woman who has no one to lean on or depend on? A woman rejected by everyone she's ever loved, wanted as a lover, or called friend?

It was like he was congratulating me for surviving annihilation.

He can call me friend, but he never acted like a friend. He claims admiration, but he's only ever dismissed me.

I believe he wrote with sincerity and pure intentions, but I received his words like a knife plunging into my heart. Such fine words twenty-two years pass any value for my life. He will be remembered most for not wanting to touch me, while he publicly fawned over a trail of women. He didn't want to be with me, yet he chased after so many others. He was so seemingly generous with his favors, I couldn't help but wonder, *"What was wrong with me that he passed me over so completely?"*

∞　　　　　∞　　　　　∞

What if we aren't made to love at all?

What if I overreached? Had too lofty of a goal to love people? What if the fact that Jesus had to die for love to be expressed in the world is evidence that love is an impossible threshold for humans to achieve in life?

I've been thinking of my love manifests that have framed my faith walk and belief or rather articulated stages of my understanding: *"Can I love you?"* and *"… the people said 'Hell no!'"* Then there was a *"Love Anyway"* stage where I took the position of love being actions that could be performed regardless of reciprocation from others. It rolls into my kindness theology which is anti-politeness (falseness, appearance) but pro-kindness and truth (honest deeds done for good). Perhaps the next installment will be *"Love, the impossible dream!"*

I want to say I'm over all of it and give up, but I'm not and I won't. However, I'm tired, discouraged, sad and lonely. I ache.

Dear Creator, is Your answer to *"Can I love you?"* to make me feel inadequate no matter how I show up or contribute? To make me feel as if my heart is not enough for anyone in this world? To show me to myself as a misfit? Unwanted. Unneeded. Unloved. For this understanding is the outcome of the lessons from my journey so far.

~ Journal: Sunday, October 23, 2022

My Three Homes: River, Gateway, Desert

Siddhartha spoke of his River as a spiritual crossing
flowing between carnal pleasures and spiritual truth
with seekers of one or the other
crossing to the designated bank

In his youth, Siddhartha crossed the River
with his purity intact. Only to discard it immediately
upon landing on the other side.

Later in life, disenchanted with worldly success
and excess, he ran back to the river,
hoping to return to what he was.
He didn't make it across.
The tranquility of the River,
lured him to stay – to flow up, down
across, ferrying other seekers of Sensuality
and Spirituality to their destination.

Siddhartha spoke of the River as
a Place existing beyond time.
The River is all things all at once.
It is up, down; ebbing, flowing, rippling and still,
deep, shallow, touching the shore and infinity
simultaneously. Everywhere the River flows,
it is fully there, present. Existing. He became the River.

Milwaukee, my river, my incubator,
my teacher, my place of transition.

Milwaukee, a city and a river on a Great Lake,
a place I've always resented, was home for sixteen years.
Returning for a short visit, after another sixteen years away,
completed a cycle of transformation. In most ways...
all ways, on the surface of my perception, the core of
Milwaukee, the nature of its people, is the same –
off-putting, limited in grace and opportunities.

Yet, at my core, I am Milwaukee. Molded and
conditioned by the city – its scarcity and potential.
Shown what could be and a path to achieve it
should my will and strength prevail.
Milwaukee took my roots, planted them deep
in nutrient-rich dirt, flooded them with rainwater,
blocked them in months of wintry darkness followed
by sun-soaked springs. It was all preparation.
I cross Milwaukee. I come. I leave.
I transition through and around
Milwaukee to get to my other places.

My next main place was New York City
my chosen home, my dream, creative fertilizer,
opportunity magnifier, gateway to transformation.

In New York, every possible sensory pursuit
is on full display, easily accessible. Whatever you
envision, is available in the *City that Never Sleeps*.
Money, fame, career, sex are basic goals.
Beware! Depravity is one step from curiosity.
Falling into temptation is like breathing.
Personal evolution, however, is a battle.

In New York, I crashed into limitations coated in glitter.
My worldly pursuit was a career leading to
financial independence. After a decade,
I finally saw the glass ceiling no one wanted
me to rise above remaining pressed between
it and the glass floor of oppression. A Black Woman,
with three degrees, working at a top global bank,
in a financial capital, was not deemed promotable
beyond Senior Executive Assistant. Trapped in
a gilded cage of stellar pay and benefits.
Oppression is hard to claim while gripping gold bars.

Yet, nothing screams injustice more than
targeted stagnation at the gateway to the world.
My presence was required to cater to

optics of great service and emotional support.
I was good enough to serve, never enough to mentor.
As a service provider to the elite, I had enough
access to see what I was barred from.

New York taught me I can enter all doors,
as long as I carry someone else's bags, or manage
their calendar, office and staff.

At the time I could not put my finger
on what was killing me.
what was degrading me
what was limiting me.
Eventually, I flew away from
what I thought would be the death of me –
unnamed depression, undiagnosed illness –
to the southwest desert to reassess everything.

Marana, my place of recalibration, my desert sanctuary
of peace and tranquility, oasis in a barren season.
The moment I turned onto Tangerine Road, the
Dove of God lit upon my entire being and senses!
Driving into the Tortolita Mountains put me at the
entry of a vision quest; reframing me as
a "little dove" in pursuit of joy.

Marana means death in Sanskrit. Fittingly, I arrived
after I gave up on the world. There, I died to all
my earthly pursuits and ambitions. My treasure
trove of hopes and dreams emptied itself there.
All laid to rest were all my former good intentions.

In my mind, I shattered both the glass ceiling of
limitations and the glass floor of oppression by
removing myself as a participant. I was able to
break the chains holding me and rip away the veil
blinding me to all the behaviors I made excuses for.
With a shout, I released myself.
With joy, I greeted a day.

Those who choose violence

Those who choose violence
over vulnerability
are ill-suited for
those who seek
peace and gentleness.

Clarity

How has my life changed
now that I'm willing
to call your petty malice
what it is?

It hasn't changed at all.
I simply keep scrolling.

How The One and The Other Panned Out

I was ready to risk my all
– life, choice, future,
body, spirit, mind
for him
for them
for either
both, at different times

They had only to say a word
or open their arms
their hearts
their minds

Release their love
willingly
to flow into me

But alas, neither were willing
to risk any part of himself

So, I collected all of me –
all the pieces, elements, memories,
strands, broken shards, rag-tag emotions
I could gather back
rearranged my thoughts, refocused my life
then I started risking my all for me

Pouring into myself has yielded
the best fruit, the most bountiful of harvests
the purest hopes and joys

To know I am both seed and bloom
descendant and ancestor
both the culmination and beginning of life
the hope, despair and manifestation of
many life cycles, as I am – with no

alterations or additions – simply
born this way – has gifted me with
multi-directional wisdom and
rooted me deeply in grace

I knew not what I was giving
away so recklessly
with gratitude, I thank those
who didn't want me
they forced me to pursue
myself, learn who I am
and what I want
they were the catalysts
for a life-long journey
that could have been derailed
indefinitely if they had
accommodated my lust

Welcome what's next

Now what?
What's the next destination?
Where will this road lead?

Write your next line.
Make a new path .
Forge a new reality.
Create a new way of being.
Breathe. Exhale. Relax. Rest.
Exist in your skin.
Listen to the silence.
Hear the thunder of your
heartbeat. Interrogate yourself.
Honor your questions and
answers as deep truths.

All possible things are doable.
Do you. Do what you love.
Do what grows you,
sparks and enhances you.
Open your mind to new ideas.
Outline alternate ways of living.
Find different bricks. Place them.
Build fantastic structures.

Welcome new versions of yourself.
Embrace different perspectives
and mind-bending concepts of who you
could be. Actively mold your evolution
with loving attention and purpose.
You're gonna change anyway;
change in the direction you want to grow.
Don't allow weariness to limit you.
You are next. You are now. You are here.

Without Reservation

I've been thinking –
perhaps I had an epiphany –
I thought of how I was willing,
begged God actually,
for the boon of being
with you. To my mind,
you were the greatest
possible gift.
Then it came to me
this desire to give, give, give,
to love you with all
my heart and mind
to worship and praise
your body with mine –
it was all wrong.
I was backwards.
I've been requesting things
which would not satisfy me
in the long run.
Yes, I want you.
Truly I want all
I've petitioned God for.
I do. I love you.
But there's something I want
more than the pleasure of
pouring my life into yours.
Something I need more
than my prayer answered.
Something I deserve more than
being a giver who receives
nothing in return.
My epiphany showed me
that more than anything I want,
I need to be loved and desired
unreservedly. It told me, you should be
the initiator and I should follow.

When you give of yourself, cover me,
pour your life into me –
those will be my true gifts.
When you choose to love me
with your heart, mind and spirit…
choose to join your body with mine in a
symphony of worship and praise…
Those are acts worthy of my devotion.

I was sitting and thinking –
what I wanted was so limiting.
What I saw would open the heavens.
My efforts have proven useless
against your inaction. So, my love,
I must back away from temptation.
I must resist the urge
to supplicate myself at your feet.
Resist my obsessive longing and
suppress the desire to shower my gifts on
a man who does not value
or reciprocate such devotion.
I must resist that part of me until
you present that part of yourself to me.
Your gifts will replenish and revive
even as your presence restores.
Your love will cover
even as your strength shelters.
When you join your gifts with mine
we will experience our greatest blessings.

You want to be worshipped

You want to be worshipped,
but don't know how to
give worship. The Creator of All
Kisses me with sunlight
Cradles me with gentle breezes
Speaks to me in silence
Feeds me wherever my feet tread
Bathes me in moon beams
Covers me in a blanket of stars
Parts oceans for my passage
Moves mountains to preserve me
If you refuse to mimic the Master
You will never master me.

It's amazing how the sun follows me

From east to west
North to south and back again
Wherever I am there it is
Rising shining setting and guiding

Even on gray days
Its muted haloed light
Spreads evenly across surfaces,
Rounding corners, softening life edges

When the clouds disperse
Startling bright beams chisel out
lines, creating sharp shadows.
The evidence of light showcases
the value of darkness.
Without darkness, what can be
appreciated in the light?
Shadows outline and enhance
To give depth and definition

Darkness itself frames light
Basking in the sun is marvelous
Respecting darkness allows perspective
Honoring both increases wisdom

I give thanks for the sun following me
each day, especially into darkest of nights

What Color Light Am I?

The sun hitting the horizon
Isn't the main event.
The show begins once the sun
is out of sight, but its
rays reach across the sky
bouncing off the atmosphere
tagging clouds, teasing out shadows.

The subtle grace and beauty of nature
reclaims my breath,
the way the sun kisses my skin,
trailing contours, brightening highlights,
caressing my melanated tones
into a reflective glow
humbles and intrigues me.
If I am a child of light, I wonder,
then, what color light am I?

Am I vibrant and stunning?
Or pale and wispy?
Does my light illuminate shadows?
Enrich textures or change
the light around me?
Am I altered or enriched
by varying degrees of nature's
radiance awakening life?
Is my luminosity visible in the
darkest night or the brightest day?
Am I a diluted wisp? Ethereal?
Or a filtered gray haze? Uninspiring?
Does my luminescence cover or expose?
Does my radiance brighten paths or
blind the unsuspecting?
What color is my brilliance?

Does my stardust twinkle

to the edges of the universe?
Am I being observed from
ninety-three billion light years away?
Am I even visible or felt at such a distance?
What do I look like from the beginning of time?
From the edge of space?
Is my shine pure white, pitch black?
A cosmic twilight blend? Vibrant purple?
Crimson red? Burning orange?
A gleaming silvery Earth moon luster?
Glowing but mellow yellow?
Bright, moderate green encouraging
voyagers to come hither?
Or is my light a color I've never seen?
Indescribable, full of majesty and awe?

What if all possible spectrums of light,
Known, unknown, seen, unseen
exists in me? What if I embody
the entire spectrum of every
life-giving electrical unit?
What if I am shining at a frequency
impossible to capture and comprehend
so, I represent only one dimension
easy to articulate in this form?
What if I am something so glorious,
destroyers will know eternal shame
for attempting to extinguish my radiance?

Knowing myself fully would leave
me awestruck; lost in the wonder of
all I AM. If I knew the color, brilliance,
frequency, reach or intensity of my light,
would I even recognize myself?
Would I have sense enough to pause, honor
or bask in my own resplendence?

Questioning Time

We are neither here nor there.
Words matter in theory,
but they are only wisps of air;
tickling sound waves.
Our eyes wide shut
or closed open
see the same illusions
pleasing to whatever lies
we tell ourselves.
Chosen reality rarely differs
from discarded options
We're all someone doing
something to be somebody
somehow taking some time
somewhere to simply be
in someone else's dream.

How far have we traveled?
Is today a day or simply
an expression of space?
Is yesterday really gone?
Will tomorrow ever come?
Can any day stand alone?
Does time even exist?
How can yesterday be
a memory when all that
was, or will be, is now?

Please, one thing before I go.

I just want to hold
on to some joy
in this world,
Father Mother
Universe Creator,
when I'm around
other people.
Keeping the joy
You've blessed me
with would be nice.

From Many Unknowns

I am LaShawnda, sister of Kim and Nicolette.
We are daughters of Terry Ann, the daughter of Bessie Mae,
the daughter of Lizzie, the daughter of Mae Emma,
the daughter of many Unknowns.

I am from bergamot grease and coconut oil;
from pinto beans and bananas.
I am from the Light of Creation,
home-cooked meals, shadowy corners, and
Thanksgiving feasts are for week-long leftovers.

I am from the weeping iris and budding tulips,
the majestic maple tree, whose thick trunk
I remember climbing up and falling down from.

I am from nowhere and everywhere.
Molded by many mothers and no real fathers.
Acclimated in violence, silence, solitude and perseverance.
Cured through imagination and hard work with spots of joy.

I am from sharecroppers and life-long toilers,
farmers, gardeners, strong women, and providers.
I've been formed through the oppression of my ancestors
the generational resilience of my grandmothers and
the unruffled pragmatism of my Mama.

I am from poor advice, "keep it in the family,"
the catch-all, "God is trying to tell you something,"
and "do unto others as you... well, just do as I say!"

I'm from stardust and grace, refined in fires of supernovas.
I'm from Gary, Indiana by way of Mississippi and Arkansas
by way of Virginia, South Carolina and Louisiana
by way of Cameroon, Nigeria, West Guinea, and Britain
by way of One Africa seeding the World.

I am from the beginning and the end.
From all that is and all there will ever be.
From salvation and damnation, prophecy and legacy
I am from abundance and sufficiency. I am existence.

He shakes all things loose

Heavy is the heart that hopes.
Shake it free of debris, lingering
remnants, shards, clusters and clots.

I would have loved so well...
Attempted to love
with my whole being.
When I believed love was
real
possible
achievable
doable
I offered myself fully,
openly to everyone.
Until belief in love was
shaken from me.
Love has proven to be
impossible
elusive
in this world
dimension
lifetime.

Actually, when has love ever
existed in human history?
The first man lied to God,
refused to trust God,
chose himself over God.
How can anyone embrace
what they reject?
Impossible.

If love was my ministry, I've failed.
Miserably. Indeed, was setup
for failure from the beginning.
When I realized no one cared for me,

it was hard to keep caring in general.
In the absence of receiving,
Nothing I had was replenished
and my rations cycled out.

Now roaming the Earth with
nearly no expectations, yet
expanding perspectives,
cleansing through empty cycles
edifying reflections while being
relationally unencumbered is
an unanticipated benefit of
being so harshly shaken.

Have I ever loved?

Who am I if not
A creature created in the
Image of love?
But what's an image
If not a facsimile?
Non-original,
Incapable of being
Authentic?
If love is the act and reaction –
We love because
We have first been loved –
Then where is the love
I'm supposed to react to?
Who forgot to pour into me?
What can I give if
I haven't received anything?
During my existence there
Have been no sheltering arms
Encouraging embraces
No partner or mate
With whom to lay down
Or to build up
What would I know
Of a gentle touch
Tender kisses
A thrusting merge
An expectant birthing
A purposeful feeding?
How am I to learn
The deep nature of
Sharing in true relationship?
When my existence
At every level
Has been solitary
Relating to myself

Even in disagreement
I am right though my
Conclusions may be wrong.
If I don't even know
What love
Looks like
Feels like
Sounds like
Smells like
Tastes like
How can I possibly
Recognize love?
Identify myself as love?
Give what I haven't received?
All these years I thought
I was offering when
I was actually begging
Trying to avoid my emptiness
Attempting to camouflage
My brokenness
Seeking to heal into wholeness
While offering my ideal image
To the broken.
But if love is absent
From my being
How was I ever whole?
How was I ever able
To offer myself at all?

It is what it is

It is what it is
Here I am
So there I be
Whatever comes
Has already gone
I was over yonder
Now I'm down under
Past present future
Only moments in time
No continuum
No parallel
Just points in orbit
Chaotic explosive
Electrifying
Patterns repeat
Moments don't
I was there
Now I'm here
Tomorrow
I'll be elsewhere
It was what it was

i wonder

i wonder what it
would have been like
to be loved
cared for
honored
protected
what would life have been
had I had someone
blatantly
obviously
courageously
in my corner
flanking me
supporting me
friending and loving me?
would I have been
different
better
happier
would I have
experienced true family
engaged in authentic
relationships
been a part of anything
worth living for?
i wonder how I would
view myself and people
encountered throughout
life if kindness and honesty
were valued in
human interactions

the blessing of ordinary

if i should happen in quite
some ordinary way
to remain
sustain or
simply maintain
my existence
i would count myself
among the extraordinary

if I should happen in quite
some ordinary way
to breathe
consistently
deeply
repeatedly
without thought
difficulty or obstruction

if i'm able to exist... like air
then certainly i'd number
among the extraordinary

we're conditioned for selfishness
immediate self-gratification
taught to despise emotion
ignore empathy
discount sympathy
without understanding practicality
taught to live in the moment
for ourselves
for what feels good
we're told self-focus
makes us extraordinary, yet
it flings us about like wisps of wind

appreciation of the ordinary

exposes abundant blessings
allowing for extraordinary
insights in a world where
we're expected to accept
what's given to us
done to us
told to us
shown to us
where we're not expected
to think for ourselves
of others or beyond
what we see, feel, want, or need

however, having learned to
grow through vulnerability
navigate darkness and greyness
unlearn toxicity
confront abusers and their enablers
having learned to love myself
embrace and accept my wholeness
reenforce my strengths
confidence and faith
basic life elements
uncommon to many
yet necessities for wellness
it's clear i've been favored

if I live to remember
a dream
loves embrace
happiness' pursuit
then the ordinary has
become a path to the divine

so many years of yearning
for extraordinary happenings
only to discover blessings
in the ordinary course days - *Asé*

Cycle of returns

Throughout the journey,
I've returned to most places.
It makes sense to return to
New York City as well.

When I get rich
An ode to $AMC

If I get rich
today,
I'm done
with all this
bullshit.

When I get rich
I'm returning
to the desert
to build a bunker
deep in the earth
far off the grid.

My fortune is
already spent on air,
sunlight and privacy.

That's it. That's my
sustainability plan.

Once a Woman Has Learned to Satisfy Herself

Is there any need for a man after
a woman learns to satisfy herself?
Does she not solve her own problems when she
learns to observe and listen to her needs?
When she learns to acknowledge, self-soothe, and
comfort herself? What need is there for an
outside voice that isn't tuned to her heart?
When a woman becomes content with her
solitude, what lure does a man have to
wiggle into the space she created?

When she realizes being alone has
its own blessings, she confronts her single -
ness practically and engage life with
clear eyes. She's less likely, at this point, to
entertain male idiosyncrasies.

When she discovers she's good with tools and
can leverage heavy things to move them,
the need for a man's physicality
diminishes. When she admits rarely
receiving the help she has requested
while unsolicited advice drowns her,
she stops missing interacting with men.

When a woman stops seeking love outside
of herself, her sense of wholeness is lost
in casual arms. Once a woman has
explored, learned, matured, and aged alone, what
value is there in coupling without shared
goals and memories? Reminisces would
unfold like highlight reels neither has real
interest in. When a woman, who has aged
beyond the use or joy of her womb, builds
her community with reciprocal
agreements, convenient exchanges, and

need-based arrangements, rest assured that the
hope-filled dreams of her youth for romantic
love with a man who'd convert her into
a wife and mother have fully soured,
shriveled into the dark depths of her soul.
Once a woman comes to terms with being
alone in a world that only honors
people in multiples, it becomes a
hardship to see a man as anything
other than a destroyer of her peace.

Where there is no lust, there is no desire,
what else then is there to want from a man?
When a woman is content living for
herself, what value can a man offer?
Companion, lover, confidant, partner,
friend, sage – she has become all to herself.

When no one has been present for any
Important event self-sufficiency
and self-reliance are defaults. Moving
forward alone is the only known way

My Three Homes: Places of Death and Life

"I don't want to die here."

I didn't want to die in New York City
so, I ran to a place I could collect myself,
rethink trajectory, focus on myself,
heal wounds, live for self.

In Marana, Arizona, a
Sonoran Desert town,
I died to my dreams and aspirations.
I died to my loneliness.
I died to my fear.
I died to all my senses,
all my hopes and ideals.
I died to myself.
The desire for everything
I once strove for died with me
in the dry brush.

Unconsciously searching for a place
of resurrection, I took a cross-country
road trip only to end up back
in Milwaukee, Wisconsin –
my habitual place or return
following every excursion into the world.

In Milwaukee, I lived with rage
I lived with angst, I lived with anger.
Yet somehow there was still an
Expectation of greatness, of growth,
for opportunity and options.
<<Insert diabolical chuckle.>>
In Milwaukee, I continued to die.

I learned again there are no safe places.
I died to the idea of financial security.

Money has no real power.
Progress and gainful employment
always depend on someone else.
My remaining long-term friendships
combusted. The illusion of closeness
persisted over the distance of
sixteen years and infrequent visits.
However, close proximity exposed
their jealousy and distain.

After a while, my rage was defeated.
I couldn't sustain it as life unraveled.
Overwhelmed by the futility of screaming
about injustices, my anger disintegrated.
I'm still dying to caring about old
mistreatments and abuses; being
taken for granted and discarded.

Surviving harsh situations, exposed constructs,
processes, systems, and lies that tied me
to harmful people, places, things, and ideas.
Those connections festered as long as I held on.
Regeneration began when I practiced letting go.

During this return to Milwaukee,
I was stripped of everything but my body,
my mind, spirit, soul and faith.
No employment, no friends, no family, no money.
Nothing to support me beyond my overall
Spiritual well-being and state of mind.

I wanted to be and do so much!
I wanted to grow, to lift, to provide.
I wanted to be a conduit of peace
and tranquility to my circles. A sharer
of knowledge and opportunities for
everyone connected to my journey.

In the end, the best I could do was die

to all of me. All the fictions I was
and storylines I outlined.

All my eager good intentions brightened
my face when I moved to New York City with a
a chest full of hopeful dreams, creative ideas,
and ambitious visions. Pregnant
with possibilities, I birthed several books,
but the true seed has yet to manifest.

Leaving the City didn't stop death
from chasing. Burial markers trail me.
Ironic, New York was the only place
I ever lived fully out loud. It was fitting
to leave to die elsewhere. New York
fleshed me out and colored me in. It framed a
greater understanding of personhood.
Being all I needed to be in order to become
the promise of the seed within. New York
was the first place I was free to explore
who I am in tandem with various interests.
Free to practice *being*. Where I first learned
to appreciate all my facets. In New York, I
lived exuberantly, fearlessly; witness to
variations of existence, opportunities
and experiences. Embraced diversity
of self, and of engaging with others.
New York City was life, but during my time
I thought of it as a spiritual desert.

In Marana, Arizona, an actual geographic desert,
I saw only life in the arid valley oasis of lush green
vegetation surrounded by a vast brown
mountainous desert. I give thanks for the
peace and tranquility in this place.
I flourished there before my body got sick.
Or perhaps my body arrived sick and the clean
dry air – that encouraged me to breathe
deeply (not the shallow breaths city dwellers

accustom themselves to), the calm environment,
soothing vistas, and my open beautiful home,
pulled impurities to the surface, forcing a purge
that shut down my system for a reboot.

How was my perception so juxtaposed? Or was it?
Maybe my understanding is lagging?
New York City: wasteland where miracles were demonstrated.
Sonoran Desert: Oasis where faith was tested and sustained.
Seeds of faith were planted and rooted in one place.
They sprouted and blossomed in another.
The process of journey flows through many places,
many moments and lessons across seemingly different lives.
In hindsight, the result of journey will show one place,
one moment, one lesson for one life cycle.

Milwaukee, place of my transition – my launch pad.
In my mind, Milwaukee had anything to offer.
I've never wanted to live there, yet it's where
the whole of my life makes the most sense.
My mother is buried in Milwaukee. My sister
refuses to leave. It's where my family
was last together under one roof.
In Milwaukee, I became a part of an
extended family as my nucleus separated.

Fast forward three decades. Milwaukee is
where everything continues to coalesce.
Where I pull at the corners of understanding,
Sweep away the ravaged remains of things
I thought I had but didn't really hold.
Milwaukee, my launch pad, my incubator
is preparing me for my next great stage.
The next place will be appreciated
it will be honored and embrace in real time.

When I asked, I received.

When I asked for courage, Abba exposed my enemies.
When I asked for strength, Jehovah gave me challenges.
When I asked for wisdom, El Shaddai graced me with adversity.
When I asked for understanding, God intensified my struggles.
For patience, Yahweh-Rapha gave me a heart for people.
For a home, El Shammah made me a constant visitor.
For financial security, Jehovah Jireh blessed me with talents.
When I pleaded for love, El Elyon revealed Himself to me.
Instead of a mate, Elohim made me a self-sufficient woman.
Instead of a family, Emmanuel guided me into solitude.
Rather than a fabulous life, Yahweh-Rohi sat me in a wilderness.
I learned that life is not about getting what we want.
El Roi guides us into becoming who we need.

Release
A prayer of letting go

I release everyone touching my life
with ill will and no good intentions.

I release people intent on siphoning
energy, faith, time, and good will.
Takers with no record of giving anything,
no practice of emotional or spiritual reciprocity,
or mutually edifying sharing will no longer
be welcomed or tolerated. Those without
care or concern for my well-being
and personhood, are released.

I release relationships I've clung to
in fear and hope, with loyal expectation.
I release visions, dreams, and ideas that
Bound me beyond their fruitful seasons.

I release people, places, things, ideas,
trauma, pain and disappointments.
Most of all, I release myself from
pursuing anything rooted in this world
with no spiritual benefit; from dead connections –
relationships that haven't born fruit
given joy or planted a seed of faith.
I'm no longer bound by anything here.
I rest in my Creator and seek to be
useful according to the Creator's purposes.

Selah.
Amen.

The Journey

The journey is hard and long.
It doesn't get easier
or shorter by staying
where you are.
Get up.
Continue forward.
You'll be glad you did.

What are you getting in exchange?

What are you getting in exchange
for access to your body, mind, spirit?
your energy, presence, time
your knowledge, skills, and resources?

What are you receiving?
for pieces of you?
Your experiences, understandings,
your vision, hopes, strategies
encouragement, and dreams?

When people pillage your mind and peace
Are you compensated for the carnage?

When others gouge you
Without refilling holes, watering moats,
smoothing ridges, bridging canyons,
when no healing recompense is offered
what do you get in exchange for open sores,
gaping wounds, scabbed scars, harm done to
lost and destroyed pieces of you?

All of life is giving, receiving
Growing, shrinking, filling, emptying,
cycling, reciprocating.
Giving or taking too much always
warps the giver and the taker.

When looters leave with no care
for damage caused, do you restock?

How do you pull yourself together?
What do you do to regain autonomy?
How do you restructure
reconstitute
realign

re-balance
re-imagine
re-envision
re-hope?
How do you remind yourself of who you are?
Dare to rethink yourself, your life, your options.
Radically reevaluate access to you. Make sure
you get what you need in exchange for
the parts of yourself left behind.

What if fear holds a truth?

Seeing you smiling
Talking, shining, happy
has always brought joy –
bursting, heart throbbing,
overflowing joy. Giddy –
I haven't felt giddy in so long.
Your smile does that.
Your voice quickens me.

How to know if you're earnest?
sincere, not playing or teasing;
seeking temporary diversion?
How to know how much to tip in?
Just a toe, both feet, my whole body,
pledge my life? Do I dare
keep risking all of me for one who
has never risked anything for me?

A fear I have rarely, if ever, articulated:
What if I can't? What if I can't be
uninhibited? What if I can't be *who*
I envision? What if I can't be the carefree
lover I so desperately need?
What if I can't cut loose the bonds
and be the loving woman I want to be?

What if I'm not the muse, but only the siren
calling forth my own destruction?
What if I can only ever be the fantasy;
never the warm, enveloping body
that nurtures and births,
receives and gives to satiate our hunger?

What if fear carries a truth?
What if that truth is barrenness,
unlovedness, rejection, lack

of ability, lack of openness?
Just *lack, lack, lack?*
Can't? Can't. *Can't!*
I hate that word! There is nothing
I cannot do, but there's so much
I cannot be. And that is a truth.

What if I'm all talk and no arch?
All eyes and no hold?
What if the writing of the vision is
better than the performance of the words?
What if, even with you, I freeze –
unable to receive, to reach back
to touch and to hold?
What if everything I've ever wanted
is sitting in the palm of my hand
and my fingers are frostbitten?
Damaged. Destroyed. Inoperable.
Unable to function.

What if you are a mirage
in the oasis of my fractured hopes?
And everything that pulls me towards you
is a figment of an imagination trapped in a loop?

What if fear holds a truth?
Perhaps the truth is so all-consuming,
fear is a subconscious defense mechanism
warning of the imminent end of me –
Solo Me, the me who is alone in the world –
the only way I've ever existed.

I write to release the fear. The truth is,
when you finally grab hold of me –
with both hands, all your heart,
mind, focus, and loving intention –
I will never let you go.

In Real Life

If I had authority with you,
you would have declared yourself,
your intentions, your life, to me long ago.
New York would maybe still be a dream
and we'd be approaching twenty years of
matrimony with teen-aged children. Perhaps.
This lost possibility is the root of my anger,
disillusionment and doubt. If love and nurture
avoided me in my youth – flushed with
so much promise, hope, and enthusiasm
why would it seek me in my aging years?
When the cycles of life are
reversing and deteriorating?

If I had any power, you would have
never been more than arms reach away,
in case I needed to be held or wanted
to hold, to cling, to disappear into you.
In all ways, for all time, you've been my constant.

If my authority and awareness of you meant
anything in this realm, real life would be
different. Yet we exist in a world where
we've breathed nearly half our lives
in different time zones and opposing realities.
Left with wispy memories of surprising
communion and brief touches. My hand
resting on your bicep in a passing greeting
(my hand has never looked so small)
Your forearms clasping at the curve
of my lower back, pulling me into
a close embrace. The residue of a
powerfully magnetic connection lingers
still – even though we haven't shared
physical space in a dozen years.

As much as I've decried this as a one-sided
attraction, trying to write it off as
only in my head, you're simply better
at resisting, camouflaging – substituting.
Like a magnetic center, my mind stays on you.
It can travel no meaningful distance
without being pulled back. Nature, balanced as it is,
tells me I must be your magnetic center as well.
Stuck in a rotation we have no control over,
or more scientifically, $F = GMm/R^2$.

"Don't walk away from me, Woman!"
will forever be the sexiest string of words
my ears could possibly hear.
"I'm not," the subtlest surrender,
a simple declaration – a promise for the ages.
Though "I can't" is more accurate.
I'm here. Present. Waiting an eternity
to be welcomed home.

I tried walking away from this deferred union.
Tried throwing myself off the shelf you placed me on,
where I reluctantly observed life passing me by.
I have no desire to know about your life
when I'm not invited to share in it.

It's interesting to know you feared a volcanic eruption
 – a loss of emotional control that could have
Incinerated everything around you –
while I feared being a doormat. So totally consumed,
by your presence, personality, and life, I simply laid myself
down at your feet. Overwhelmed, but quietly accepting.

What if our fears held our truths? What if both
fears were – are still – valid and survivable?

What if your scorched earth is a way to prepare
the ground for new growth? Rebirth?
Rejuvenation? A new way of thinking and being?

What if my doormat vision was simply
surrender and supplication? An invitation
for you to join me in posture and heart?

What if I can think of no better place to be
than at your feet, *a la* Ruth, should you choose
to lay yourself down with me, *a la* Boaz?

Sunset Crater Volcano is one the most beautiful places
my eyes have seen. The cratered mountain is covered
by pitch black lava-covered earth. The flourishing
re-populated forest, which had to break through
incinerated earth encrusted with thousand-year-old
lava rock, stands as witness to the true force of life.
The nutrient-rich scorched earth is evidence
of its volatile nature. The well-nourished
flora and fauna, are the truth of love.
The whole volcano is a fantastic display
of certain death and absolute life.
An evolutionary cycle.

I'm not scared of you. Erupt. Usher in your next era.
Perhaps it will include me, maybe it won't.
Your existence has enriched me with nutrients
found only in the fire of longing. Life being what it is,
I'll keep growing through the crevices toward the light.

On some level, in some dimension, we are
already One, we've never been parted. Our
Intentions have always been clear, and pure.
Direct, honest communication. Somewhere
we've already figured this out in real life.

Confident to be me

I'm a slow starter,
a leisurely getter.
Steady, focused
meticulous and determined.
I know what I want.
I know what's good for me.
I know me.
What gives me pleasure,
purpose, energy,
encouragement and motivation.
I'm my loudest and most
consistent cheerleader.
My greatest supporter, showing
up for myself, by myself.
Being present for self,
is the best expression of self-love.
I'm a lover and a giver –
open, honest, genuine,
authentic, loyal, and faithful.
A vessel and conduit seeking
to pass on, untainted, what's
been so generously poured into me.
Thank you, Father, Mother, Universe, Creator,
for the care You have taken with me.
Thank you for the ability to move confidently
in the love You've nurtured me in.

Absence of Trust

Tr*uth* finally confronted me
while advising a friend.
It showed me roots and connections
Like a red ball bouncing through
Memories of trauma-stunted development

Of all the men who have impacted my life –
some of whom claimed to love, admire,
or want me; desired to possess me,
my presence, energy, attention, or focus –
none were actually safe, attentive,
or interested in my well-being.
They provided no physical protection,
emotional shelter, or spiritual cover.
No man has ever been a harbor for me.
Not dad, grandpa, any uncle, brother, cousin, or friend.
None of the coaches or managers,
coolest coworker or fevered crush.
The best of them were simply there,
never present, only manspreading across space.
Hovering. Menacing. Hunting. Poisoning their surroundings.
The worst were absolute destroyers – devastating lives,
families, futures – inflicting trauma they learned.
They were predators, controllers, haters,
saboteurs, takers, users, empty promise makers.

That bouncing red ball...
Remember Peewee and his brother?
Remember the uncle you told who
kept silent because it wasn't his business?
Remember your confusion about identity,
Worthiness, sexuality, desire, and connections?
Family? If you can't sleep in peace at home,
where can you ever be at peace?
Oh, that bouncing red ball!
Setting off catalysts of memory.

Violated, but so naïve. Am I, or aren't I?
Never a virgin. Never experienced
Far too worldly, yet ridiculously clueless.
Growing into womanhood, running from suitors;
Chasing philanderers – smooth-talkers cosplaying
suitable catches. My sight has always been skewed.
My hope was first deeply planted in despair.
I never stood a chance. Life was never going to be normal.
Trust has always been absent and foreign.
Never nurtured. Never rooted.

Though not one to blame myself
for the violence or neglect of men
I have wondered if I'm too resistant to engage
in a way they understand. I communicate interest,
but don't grab hold. Reach, but don't connect fully.
Guess I thought it was me. Perhaps my inability
to partake in cultural mating practices was due
to being damaged or broken. Or the trauma clinging
like tattered skin, no matter how healed I think I am.

While bouncing a red ball along my friend's memories
I shared a story about a man who went without his
glasses all day. He waited for his girlfriend to get home
from work so she could help him look. She found
his glasses in the first place she checked –
the bathroom – his first stop in the morning.

Incredulous, I said to her,
> "If a man can't be trusted to do the simplest thing for
> himself, how can he be trusted to lead you in life?"

While telling this story in relation to my friend's
failed marriage and my never-launched ships,
the loudest a*ha* echoed.

To my friend, I said:
>   *"If I can't trust him with my vulnerability –*
>   *trust him with my truth, my feelings,*
>   *my honesty, my desire – how can I possibly*
>   *trust him with my body... or my life?"*

And just like that, I knew what's been holding me back!
>   *No man has ever been trustworthy*
>   *for the tiniest thing. Not dad, not grandpa,*
>   *uncle, brother, cousin, or friend. The best*
>   *were nonchalant. The worst were monsters.*

I've never been emotionally safe with anyone.
Even well-intentioned women told me how
to feel while shaming me for my truth.

If a man enjoys creating confusion and uncertainty;
hurting, dismissing, or ignoring my feelings –
if he's indifferent to the emotional harm he inflicts –
the truth is, he has no respect for my personhood.
It's impossible then for him to honor me in my totality.
The absence of honor leads to an absence of trust.

My spirit knew this, but the world in me was stubborn.
Ego wants what it wants, yet Joy only accepts Joy.
Trust seeds in honesty and clarity; it roots
in consistency. Truth will only go where
Truth resides. Finding no worthy reflection
in the world, Joy holds to itself, Truth
becomes tainted, and trust disappears.

PART 5: LEARNING TO TRUST MYSELF AGAIN

I Already Do

During my young adulthood, I put so much trust in connections I thought I had with people, that I not only weighed my worthiness, I balanced my understanding of my faith, by their response to me. Their lack of reciprocal care made me doubt my understanding – of instructions, guidance, teachings, messages – even up to the foundation of my faith. My recovery from this dreadful lapse of trusting my intuition, my hearing, my heart, my eyes and my hopes was to push it all into the shadows and trust only what I could confirm as God's guidance. This proved to be quite an over-correction on my part.

The loss of so many imbalanced relationships – with people I held dear as friends and family or would have gladly called lover – paved the way to my withdrawal and isolation. Throughout my forties, I've actively resisted making new friends and aggressively shooed men away. What I'm understanding now is, I stopped trusting my sight. Not only did I have visions, I also had eyes filled with hope and love – natural filters that cover a multitude of sins.

Now, I see people as they are in a world I don't want to be a part of. This includes seeing myself as I am, in all my flawed, fragile humanity. A new understanding is forming: despite my unwillingness to see people through filters of hope and love, I need to trust that it's still necessary to practice doing so. I need to trust that my deficiencies are not limitations when I allow God to work and love through me.

When will I trust myself again? Trust myself to open up, despite the inevitability of disappointment, without sliding further into isolation? Trust myself to see with refreshed eyes of grace instead of through the residue of all the false relationships in my life? Trust myself enough to protect myself in any environment without concern for retaliation?

I already do. That work has already been done.

The beauty of being able to see people as they are, is that the little power they have in subterfuge is taken away. When truth is spoken into a deceitful person's face, they have no idea how to respond. They usually double-down or back down. Either way, they know they are exposed. Truth takes away the *go-along-to-get-along* cushion they're used to when they dangle carrots to control performance within their environments. Nope. That's no longer an option with me.

I've come through the testing stages with layers of grit I never asked for. I wanted to be soft, caring, trusting and full of grace, but the people in the world keep trying to break me down and chew me up. So, My Provider began training me in courses that have incrementally toughened me. Knowing I am equipped to stand in victory makes trusting myself so much easier.

~ *"Learning to Trust Myself Again."*
Harvest Life Blog, 2023

Revolution 49

My 49th birthday was a quiet day
I kept my own company and
Spoke only to order food.
And to greet neighbors.
And to sing Happy Birthday
in front of a candlelit
cake and potted orchids.
It was a good day.

Another day, another year.
A trip around the sun sounds quaint;
But 49 revolutions feel legendary.
For one, I can't envision being 49!
Where does time disappear to?
Secondly, this annual trip is
584 million miles.
In my 49 Earth years,
I've traveled more than
28.6 billion miles.
49 years may take a while to sync,
but I certainly feel the wear and
tear of all my billions and billions
of miles traveled.

Forgiveness

Forgiveness is a road
a process, a hardship, really.
At first, to forgive can seem
Like a gift of leniency.
An undeserved pardon when
one is shattered from disillusionment,
betrayal, abandonment, rejection,
neglect or abusive assaults.
A pulverized darkened heart
has no strength to love those who
worked diligently to destroy it.

> *But self-protection*
> *But space*
> *But distance*
> *But absence*
> *But time*
> *But solitude*
> *But reflection*
> *But purposeful healing*
> *But the Holy Spirit*
> *But Yeshua*
> *But God*

Bit by bit, these *buts* quiet the spirit
soothe the pain, calm the mind,
erase memories, redirect energy
repurpose life. After a while,
forgiveness is not only possible,
it's a shrug. A nonchalant grace.
It's release. A pronouncement of
freedom from the Pain Giver.
Forgiveness is

> *goodbye*
> *I'm done*
> *no more grudges*
> *no more access*
> *it doesn't matter*

I've become who
I am and I am well.
Thank you for your
contribution to my journey.

Once the pain is released,
the Pain Giver is powerless.
Moving beyond the prison of pain
allows for effortless breathing
providing the expanse to become.
My pain transmuted into strength,
purpose, perspective, understanding,
wisdom, compassion, and seeking.
It became the love filter I observe
the world through. A well of empathy
I dip into when confronted with the
callousness, dismissiveness, hubris,
and inhumanity of bullies and abusers.
I don't cower. I don't retreat. I stand.
Perhaps parry. Certainly, stare them
in the eye so they see what I see:
Someone attempting to pass
their inadequacies off to me.
Impossible to fearmonger when
you can no longer instill fear.

It's a blessing to go in peace.
Forgiveness is often the only love
A healing heart can offer.
Fare thee well, is protective prayer.

No more ·What ifs?·

I've done everything
I thought I should do.
Gone every place
I wanted to go.
Lived the dreams,
lived the horrors,
lived the sorrows.
I've chased, begged, yearned
I've shown up, contributed
and gave what I could.
I tried – oh, how I tried
to be the girl
the daughter
the sister
the granddaughter
the niece
the woman
the friend
the mate
the selection
the choice
more than an option,
the best of love,
a chosen participant
in many lives
I tried. Now I'm done.
It's a relief to be done trying
to attract love and people!

No more structuring plans on *what ifs*.
Contentment resides in just being.
Simply existing in moments as I am.
Enjoying things for what they are, where
they are, while cultivating what's been
planted for better growth opportunities.

For My English 10 Class | Class of 2026

People will use your trauma
To keep you down
Keep you bond
Keep you dependent
Keep you focused on pain
Fear
Anger
Hatred
Those who encourage your
Helplessness
Seek to control you the most
Be alert
Be ready
Be protective
Of your growth
Your life
Your hopes
Your dreams
Question
Why someone wants
To do everything for you
Make class easy
Give you things you haven't worked for

What's your story if you never learn
from experiences? Never hurt?
Never feel? Never heal and recover?
What have you accomplished
If someone can tell you
They did everything for you?
Your voice is the gateway to your life.
Use it.
Say who you are.
Be who you are.
Improve yourself daily.
Your story becomes multi-faceted

with each new tangent –
Good bad happy or sad
Everything in your life builds you
Into the person you are
Becoming
Be intentional
Be mindful
Be aware of the fact that
Who you are today is not
All you will ever be
But you have to feed your future
Self something to grow on.
Start now by writing the story
you want to become.

Thank You, Lord

Thank You, Lord, for
bringing me to this point today.
Thank You for not leaving me
where You last placed me.
Thank You for the fire and cleansing.
Thank You for pain and healing.
Thank You for the storms, the dry
desert stretches, and long dark nights.
Thank You for the overcoming,
bringing me through, and making me
battle-ready in this warring world.
Thank You for teaching me to stand.
Thank You for respite.
Thank You for my talents and work.
Thank You for peace and grace,
Thank You for keeping me.
loving me and guiding me.
Thank You for victory.
Amen.

My All In One

Thank you for continuing
to bring me back
in a disconnected,
unstable world
lacking permanence.
You repeatedly return me
to You – my Father,
Mother, Creator.
My True Self.
My All In One.

Rethinking "The One or The Other"

For many years
I thought returning would
Lead to finding and securing a mate
The One in my mind
Was the dream, the fantasy
The epitomic manhood to my womanhood
The Other was equal in possibility
delivering different types of joy,
attraction and connection –
options, so I thought.
There was an illusion of choice.
At an appointed time
In an appointed place
Man #1 or Man #2
Would I go left or right
Did I choose for spirit and connection
Or for physical and visual joy?

So many years have passed
In anticipation of being
confronted with this choice
Of standing with my heart and
arms open to two men
Years of longing
Decades of hoping
A lifetime of waiting
For *One* or the *Other*.

Today, it crossed my mind
As I sat lakeside
Pondering my fullness
Marveling at life cycles and processes
Wondering in amazement at
God's goodness in structuring and
Seasoning my life

"What if I AM *The One*?"
What if I am the person
I've been waiting for, hoping for,
dreaming of – anticipating with
all my heart, mind and soul?
What if *The Other* are those
I said "no" to when I chose myself?
Chose my comfort, equilibrium,
My safety, my peace, my solitude.
What if every man I've ever wanted
was only ever *The Other*,
because they didn't see
or choose me as their *One*?

What if I am truly enough or my life?
What if no one is missing?
What if I lack nothing and
have everything as I AM?
What if I am *The Only One* I need?

I Am.
I Am All.
I AM ALL IN ONE.
I EXIST HERE FULLY AS ONE.

Selah.
God is Good.

Beauty

One of the most beautiful experiences
in life is being able to see beauty
in all things and each stage of life.
Each one of us can reflect on the
beauty of our youth,
but how awesome to be able
to enjoy the beauty in our aging!

Like a Saguaro

Stalwart, stately, majestic
Steely frame, thorny
Hazardous skin
Shelter and nourishment
In a hostile landscape
Towering despite shallow roots
Blossoming and bearing fruit
With the bear minimum
Like a saguaro
I stand firm in the desert
rare, tranquil, beguiling,
Thriving in the right environment

Motion is Life

Water is equilibrium.
Wherever I go, find water
to sit by, to recharge
to reflect, to commune,
The roar of oceans,
expanse of Great Lakes,
flow of rivers and
rippling ponds remind me:
Motion is everything.
I'm only anchored for as long
as I want to be.
My true nature is free-flowing
beyond visible sight.
Designed as part of a limitless Creation
I too am a drop in the ocean
a gust of wind, a star in the cosmos.
Life is constant motion,
greater than we can comprehend.
Even when we think we're stuck,
motionless, going no where,
we're moving through the universe
at 228 miles per second! Traveling a
mindboggling 823,192.56 miles
per hour as stardust on the Earth!
Even on your slowest and smallest
days, you're a magnificent speedster!

I Found Me in All My Places

Milwaukee – the good earth –
has been a place of transitions –
agitating my flux and uncertainties,
angst and frustration.
Functioning as an incubator,
feeding and launching me
repeatedly onto great futures.

Paris – that city of light and love –
brought me to my knees to
kiss the ground when I first landed.
Oh! To be in my dreamland before
I knew dreams as premonitions.

New York – the city that never sleeps –
was my Dream of dreams.
It showed me the heights of life
from the mountainous peaks of skyscrapers.
It's a doorway to the world, every
imagined destination a flight away.

Marana – that a thicket of death –
centered me. Tutored me in peace and
goodwill to myself. Forced a slowdown
and rest. Allowed space to cultivate a
quiet spirit and mind. Leading to inner
calmness, ease throughout my being.

Alkebu-lan – Afrika – the Motherland
Ancient, vast rich, diverse and mysterious.
New York to Morocco on the
Way to Egypt and from Ethiopia,
Two Motherland nations named in
Genesis, connected by the
beginning and end of River Nile.
My first homeland destinations

were chosen to feed starved
embers of knowledge, of seeking to
understand ancient ancestors,
ancient histories, borders, and maps.
Fanned the desire to seek knowledge.
What is the Motherland's perspective
of its Diasporic children? What is taught
about those taken away in chains?
Needing to know more – my name, language,
tribe, DNA, homelands, pre-colonial faith systems –
builds a desire to return, return again and
continue returning until I gather each part
of me scattered around the world.

I found Me in these places. Each location
developed me more into the Woman I Am.
Each place pulled something out of me.
Exposed elements, forged remnants,
solidified "home." Each place is part of
the composite of *My Place* –
representing where I saw Me, found Me
chose, engaged and pursued Myself –
They form the framework of the
house I carry everywhere, my home within.
Every place I've been made me
more at home within Myself.

The Love Chapter

I've always wanted to
write a love story.
Unfortunately, when pen touches paper,
my tortured soul free-flows without
filter, form, or subtleties. It spews raw
emotion. All-encompassing, unsolicited
Unappreciated pain, loneliness,
sadness, rejection, frustration,
All the feelings I prefer not to
claim as part of my present reality, my story.

A summary of my existence
Sitting heavy where they landed.
Perhaps the painful feelings will never
be fully rooted out.
As long as the residual can be reprocessed
And the memories repurposed.

The romance I tried to write at 18
is forming on its own at 48.
Perhaps love needed a path clear of obstacles.
My vision of love needed time to grow into itself.
Space to form, experience to weed out toxic
dead things intent on strangling new things.
My soul needed to cleanse itself.
God-willing, my newly content soul
will have much to declare through
the upcoming Love Chapter.

Driving Timothy: By and By

Timothy got in the back seat with an anxious greeting.
"I'm late for my doctor's appointment. Can you get there fast?"

I rarely rush by request while driving.
"How you doing," I asked, eased into traffic.

"I'm doing good," he said. "Things will get better by and by."

"Do they really," I asked.

"By and by," he repeated with a weary sigh.

By and by, I reflected. "Earlier today," I said,
    I overheard a young woman lament
    turning twenty-five. She said she was
    having a quarter-life crisis. I chuckled
    as I walked past her. Then I turned around
    with a smile, 'Quarter-life crisis? Baby, God bless!'

"Oh, I know you're gonna tell me it gets better" she said.

"Well, no, I wasn't going to say that."

She goes "I know… all the fun is right now."

I told her, "I wasn't gonna say that either.
It's best not to look at life as 'fun' or 'no fun,'
'good' or 'bad.' Better to look at life and aging
as a process of *filtering*. As you age, you filter
out unnecessary things. Filtering leads to wisdom.

"At some point you're going to think about
things that come towards you in terms of:
*Do I need it? Do I want it? Do I want to spend
my time, energy or money on it?*
As your birthdays pass by, you'll see

Your answer will be "no" more often than 'yes.'
Time teaches how to filter out the unnecessaries.
That, my dear, is wisdom. Happy Birthday!"

Timothy said, "Ain't that right! Girl! You said it!"

"Thank you, Timothy! It was a word for me too!"
We chuckled, then I continued. "I used to cry
about the people who left my life and now
I don't even ask 'why.' I just keep it moving."

He chortled again, "That's a word! That's a word!"

"I've thought about it. God is so very gracious!
He moved me from tears and clutching tight to folks,
to separating me fully and accepting isolation.
What used to take years, is mostly a bat of the eye now.
I've learned to walk away. Close doors.
Stop responding and engaging.
I don't know why relationships end,
but God knows why.
I know who I am.
I know whose I am
I know the God I serve.
I know His provision and His care.
This is enough for me.
By and by!

A shared shout of thanksgiving erupted from us.

I never thought I'd shrug at losing relationships.
My deepest craving was for a good partner, children,
family, friends, community. Now, I can shrug
at not having any of it while looking forward
to a future where I am my own best friend,
my own best partner, my own best mate,
guided in all things by the Spirit of Light, Love
and Creation with care and purpose.

What a journey! By-and-by!
Becoming One with Life.
One with my Creator.
One within Myself!
No divided personality,
ideas, or commitments.
No more separation from self,
peace, joy or purpose.
I'm eliminating everything
attempting to steal me from myself.

I stopped listening. I closed my ears.
It turns out, allowing that break
taught me to listen better.

I've learned to filter my hearing, my sight.
I lamented for years the repetitious nature of life
not wanting to repeat prior experiences.
Cycles, spirals, repetition – with each level
I ascend to, recycle into, return to – every stage,
refines my filter, enhances wisdom.
Enriches sight, hearing, and discernment.
Life has been full of blessings, by-and-by!
I've become a blessing, by and by.

Woman. You Are Enough.

Woman, you are enough. Today. Right now. As you are.

Without or with children. Without or with a partner. Without or with family or friends. On your own, with only your skin and everything within, you are enough. Your value is not based on your roles, your presentation or how you show up for others. If you were to produce or perform nothing else for the rest of your days, you are still all you need for everything going forward.

Dear Woman Who Mothers:

You are equipped to provide all the true necessities for yourself and your family.

Despite what you may think, your love will never fail your children. You will always be a light to them, even in the deepest darkest pits they may fall into, everything you represent will be a beacon to them.

Your strength is phenomenal. Even in your weakest moments, your children will look back and view you as the epitome of EVERYTHING. The personification of strength and a safe harbor.

You can do wrong, but no wrong will outweigh your love. Remember that. Give yourself a break when you're overwhelmed.

You don't need to go beyond yourself to be the best mommy ever. You are already her! You are the mom your child is blessed with. Know that. Embrace it. Govern your household with this awareness.

You are a blessing. You are a lover. A nurturer. A builder. A teacher. A guide. A comforter. A savior. A survivor. You are the first true sacrifice and offering your child will ever encounter. You are the first environment of creation your child will ever experience on Earth. Your body, the most sacred of temples, hosted and presented life to the world. How awesome is that?

Your life is the largest influence your child will have. In the midst of your everyday, this may be a lot to think about. So, don't think about it. Just live. Be who you are. Do the best you can, accepting that your best varies depending on countless variables. Whatever your best is in any given moment is enough. Who you are in every moment, is enough. However you show up, is enough.

Dear Woman Who Journeys Alone:

You live in a world that values youth and views your body as a tool of production. This society that focuses on the aesthetic of your appearance and dismisses any substance in your character. By the time you understand that others value you for elements not representative of your wholeness or your truth, you will have a lifetime of learning to unlearn. Put in the work to purge yourself of the world's ideas of femininity. Make the effort to let go of what men want from the women they intend to dominate and impregnate. It will take a lot of courage to let go of the lies, false narratives and impossible goals you were given. Goals that required you to set yourself aside for the benefit of everyone else.

Woman, you are everything you need for a well-lived life. You carry a multitude of seeds within you. Not every seed is intended to be a human child. Whether you have birthed a version of yourself through your womb or not, you will most certainly birth versions of yourself through your work, words relationships, and passions. Your body is of the Earth and your mind networked to the universe's network. There is nothing you can conceive which you cannot figure out. What you figure out, you're able to create. The power to create something from a thought is a gift to humans. The ability to incubate and multiply gifts is unique to womanhood.

For whatever duration you are alone in your travels, be content. Cultivate peace. Find and hold tranquility. Be gentle with yourself. Explore your generosity and tenderness for who you were and who you're becoming. Love who you are, where you are. Every stop along your route has something to glean for your future self. Life teaches in layers, cycles and spirals. Time rarely allows us to go back for what we missed. Soak in everything you can. Collect the lessons. They will increase wisdom, endurance and grace.

As we age, it may feel as if life removes options from us. In fact, our focus and tolerance narrows. We become more protective of our resources and less willing to engage in harmful or confusing activities. Our time and energies are better managed, selectively distributed and shared.

In American society, aging is the boogeyman. In life, aging is a continuous transformation. Day after day, year after year, relationship after relationship, we are sharpening understanding, refining skills and sloughing off dead things.

Life doesn't' have to be a race, a checklist or a series of unending days full of unmet yearnings. All the joy a life can hold can be received by breathing fresh air, greeting a sunrise, walking towards a sunset, or dancing in moonlight.

We are wonderfully created beings connected to the power flowing through nature. Embrace your process. Appreciate your solitude. Though you may travel through the world alone, all you need is within you. Respect the glory of being fully self-sustaining as you are. You lack nothing. You were birthed in a universe you have a full connection to. Your power is unlimited in human terms. Be certain not to limit yourself.

I asked to be a Lover

I asked to be a Lover.
The Great Teacher made my life
a master course on caring for myself.
In sickness, health, scarcity, and abundance,
I've learned to hear my voice in noise and voids;
remain steady through chaos and calm;
reflect and analyze my light and darkness equally.

I asked to be a Lover of People.
The Creator of ALL taught me how to love myself
as a being molded by the Spirt of Love,
as Their image-bearer and vessel of breath, life and light.

I asked to be a Lover, and my Mother, Father,
Creator, Teacher taught me how to love ME as
They love me. How to settle for nothing less than
tenderness, gentleness, consideration and truth.
The Great Spirit made me a Lover of Myself.
Perhaps this is a step towards genuinely loving others.

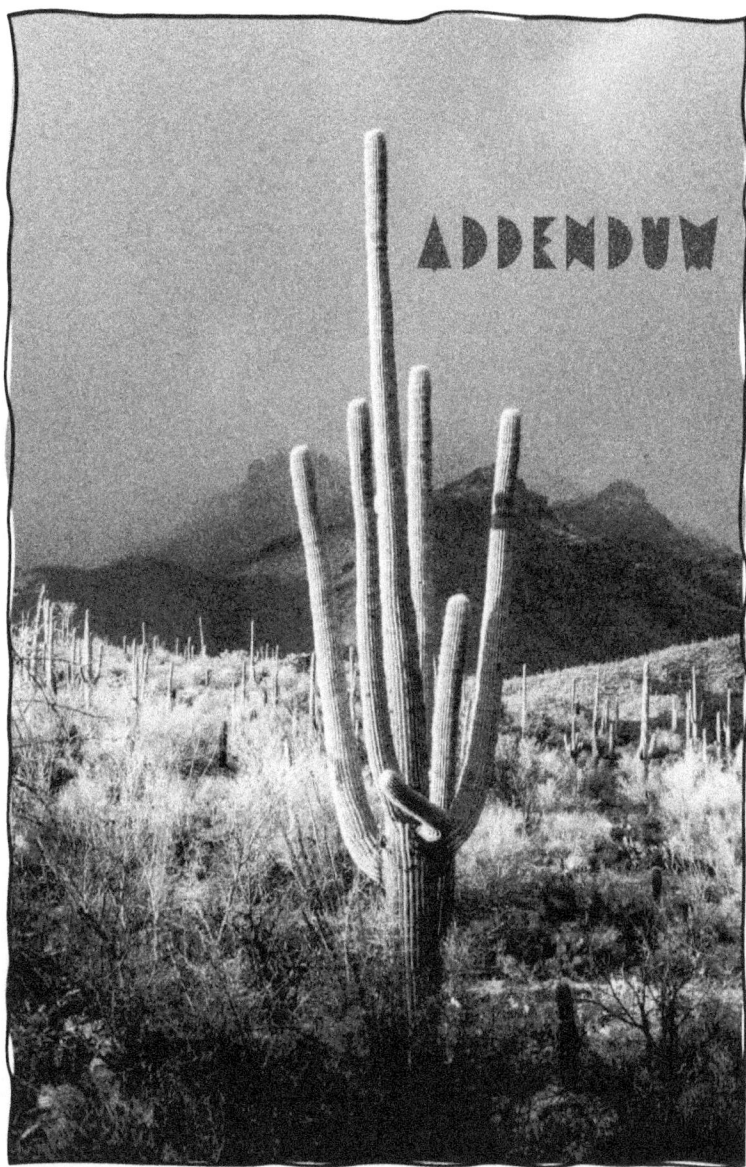

ADDENDUM

Love Anyway 50 Lessons from My Harvest

1. People's judgment of me is not my issue.

2. Rejection has never broken me, nor will it ever.

3. The world's example of love is not the love I live by.

4. Grace is not an excuse for wrong behavior.

5. Mercy is not a free ticket to take people for granted.

6. When God dwells within, not only are you unbreakable, you're unstoppable.

7. My heart may lead me wrong, but God will not. He always brings me back to where I need to be.

8. I may not always be right, but with my heart set on God, I know He'll work everything out for my good.

9. Faith, hope, and love remain. Love is the greatest, but each is co-dependent.

10. I am a blessing to everyone I encounter. You too are a blessing. We may not realize it or act like it, but it is a fact.

11. When God pruned and weeded people out of my life, the desire to chase after them disappeared. I've learned to allow Him to perform His Word.

12. I believe in God. I am not God. My response to being mistreated may not resemble your idea of love, grace or mercy, but God has tempered me.

13. My walk with God is unlike anyone else's. It's okay if other people don't understand me or my process, they are a similar mystery to me.

14. Solitude and loneliness have strengthened me in ways I never imagined.

15. In my solitude, I've been eagerly willing to obey God. In my quietness, I've my faith has increased, my joy has spread, and my self-awareness has deepened.

16. Being alone is hard, but it's also the best way to hear God clearly and intimately.

17. A pure heart is better than good intentions.

18. Intentions without action aren't worth talking about.

19. When I grow up... wait... I am grown, and still growing.

20. Those who hide themselves will entice you to live in the shadows with them. Hug tightly to the light.

21. The brighter your light shines, the more opposition you attract. Resist hiding your light. Your opposition will disappear.

22. People will resent your light. Shine anyway.

23. Once you commit to being your best self, you'll attract people eager to provoke the worst out of you. Commit to being better anyway. Resisting adversaries will strengthen you.

24. The most destructive adversaries are those closest to us. Resist the darkness within your circles and yourself.

25. Friends and family will attempt to sabotage your walk. Keep moving forward; they will fall to the wayside eventually.

26. Abusers will cry loudest about your lack of charity when their abusiveness is confronted. Confront them anyway.

27. Every attack of the enemy is intended to destroy your faith. Resist. Stand firm. Then continue moving forward.

28. A jerk by any other name is still a jerk... even when they claim Jesus and quote scripture.

29. When your faith flounders and doubt overwhelm you, hold on to whatever you can until you get through. You will be refreshed.

30. People will ridicule your faith. Build your faith anyway.

31. I may not be better than my haters, but their envy is confirmation that I make better choices.

32. People will hate you. Let them. They cannot deny your greatness.

33. The biggest challenges in your life are all the same lesson presented in various degrees, dimensions and perspectives. Get knowledge. Get understanding. Evolve.

34. Wanting the best for someone isn't as important as them wanting the best for themselves.

35. We are all free to live as we want. Make sure your free will doesn't contradict or shame your faith.

36. It's essential to let God do His crippling work in your heart and spirit. His processes will disable the power of sin in your life.

37. People will take advantage of your kindness. Be kind anyway.

38. Anger, exhaustion and disappointment are part of the journey. So are rest and recovery.

39. The last person standing has no one to lean on. Don't worry. God has you.

40. When you can encourage yourself, the lack of encouragement from others is not devastating.

41. Bitterness may occasionally overwhelm you. Immerse yourself in sweetness

42. Living for Christ is a process I hope to get right one step at a time.

43. You will grow exceedingly weary. Rest as needed.

44. God sacrificed His Firstborn Son. He understands pain and struggle.

45. I am a creation of the Most High. He is my shield.

46. Jesus wept. He understands sorrow.

47. Jesus loved. He understands longing.

48. Joy-stealers will remark on your fallen countenance. Keep radiating joy and shame the thieves.

49. Your joy will be attacked. Rejoice anyway.

50. Your love will often be rejected. Love anyway.

About LaShawnda Jones

Image by Deidre Wilson, Las Vegas, 2014

LaShawnda Jones is an observer who documents in words and images. As an independent author/publisher for *Harvest Books* and independent photographer for *Harvest Photo*, LaShawnda's work focuses on women, spiritual growth, social justice and the beauty of everyday life. Through themes of love, relationships, self-discovery, spirituality and social commentary, she shares her thoughts, experiences, and reflections. Her choice mediums are blogging, books, calendars, art prints, greeting cards and t-shirts.

LaShawnda has been journalling since she was six years old. By twelve, she was writing short stories on a seven-line Brother Word Processor.

For her eleventh birthday, she received a Vivitar 110 point and shoot camera which marks the beginning of her love for candid photography. In late 2014, she became passionate about photographing demonstrations, marches and protests. In 2021, she released her first photo essay book, *I AM WOMAN: Expressions of Black Womanhood in America.*

Alone | All in One is LaShawnda's third poetry collection and seventh book. Each element of the book is her work. All the cactus photography is from her time in Marana. The cover design and manuscript came together in Milwaukee.

LaShawnda grew up in the Midwest, in several spots around Lake Michigan and Mesa, Arizona. She matured during fourteen years in New York City followed by three mellowing years in Marana, Arizona. In 2021, she returned to Milwaukee, WI where she attended high school and college.

For more information about LaShawnda Jones, her blog, books, and photography, please visit **Harvest-Life.org** and **Harvest-Photo.org**.

CONNECT
HarvestLife2020@gmail.com

Instagram
@HarvestBooks1
@HarvestPhoto1

Threads
@HarvestBooks1

BLOGS
Harvest-Life.org
Harvest-Photo.org
LaShawndaJones.wordpress.com
AmericaRisingBlog.wordpress.com

BOOKS
Alone | All in One: A Solitary Journey
I AM WOMAN: Expressions of Black Womanhood in America
Desert of Solitude: Refreshed by Grace
My God and Me: Listening, Learning and Growing on My Journey
The Process of Asking for, Receiving & Giving Love & Forgiveness
Clichés: A Life in Verse
Fantasies: Wide Awake

Buy Books
Amazon
BN.com
Harvest-Life.org/shop

CALENDARS
VoLux Full-Figured Calendar, 2005, 2007 *(out of print)*

PHOTO ART PRINTS
Harvest Life Store on Square